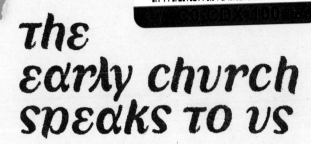

the early church speaks to us

DAILY DEVOTIONS AND BIBLE STUDIES

by H. S. Vigeveno

G/L
REGAL
BOOKS
TM

A Division of G/L Publications
Glendale, California, U.S.A.

© Copyright 1970 by G/L Publications
Printed in U.S.A.

Published by
Regal Books Division, G/L Publications
Glendale, California, 91205, U.S.A.

Library of Congress Catalog Card No. 76-104083
SBN 8307-0060-9

Contents

Foreword

1. When the Fire Falls   **1**

2. The Secret of Awakening   **15**

3. Open the Door
   and Get Out of the Doorway   **29**

4. The Dynamics of Explosion   **41**

5. The Dynamics of Conversion   **55**

6. When the Fire Spreads . . .   **69**

7. What Is Your Gospel?   **81**

8. Pagan World, Here We Come   **93**

9. The Newness of the New   **107**

10. Of a Church Awake   **119**

11. Facing Controversy   **131**

12. Wake Up, Christian!   **143**

13. The Gospel of Hope   **155**

This book may be used as an elective Sunday School course, or for Sunday evening fellowships or midweek Bible study classes.

A teaching and discussion guide for use with this book is available from your church supplier.

Foreword

You never run into any trouble when you begin a conversation on what's wrong with the church. Why? Because there's plenty that's wrong.

It wasn't always that way. Nor does it have to remain that way now. A renewal can take place. Awakening is needed. But—how does it happen?

Study the dynamics of the early Christians. What made them so successful? What moved them into all that pagan world? What brought them into such prominence that we still go back to their fellowship as our prime example for the church?

This book explores these questions. It is a student book based on an adult course, called "The Story of God and His People—God Acting Through His Church." It is an intensive study of major passages from the book of Acts and the New Testament letters.

There is of course no *one* answer to the question of renewal. But surely such a search as this which explores the phenomena of conversion, awakening, witness and missions is vital for our times. And crucial in this adventure is the power of the Holy Spirit.

Each chapter opens with a short introduction and closes with an equally short page for decision. In between are seven devotional readings (for each day of the week) based on Scripture passages. As you develop the consistent habit of reading and meditating in prayer, you may be surprised about the renewal that can take place in you!

There is no room for impotent Christianity in our world, nor is there a demand for dull, matter-of-fact Christians. People want the real thing. And that's what this book hopes to accomplish, by the grace of God and in the power of the Spirit.

CHAPTER 1

When the Fire Falls

We live in a real world of greed, trouble, conflict, hatred and rejection. The other day a Christian, who is very much in the world of hard reality, asked over the dinner table:

"Why is the church so ineffective? This is a time when many people I know are asking questions of meaning. They've lost their way. They have no direction. They really want to know. And the church doesn't seem to speak to them at all. . . ."

I had to agree that far too few people between the ages of twenty-five and forty-five seem to be a part of the church. Why not? What's wrong with us? What can we do about it?

Maybe we can't change all Christians, but we can begin with ourselves!

Introductory Bible reading for this week: Acts 1:1–2:42

We have acquired more physical power than any other people before us. And we have obtained more physical comforts than ever before. But we have also proved to ourselves that all this comfort and efficiency has not given us a meaning of life.

The real problem of man is not in his outer world, but in his inner spirit. It is not in things but in himself.

Man cannot save himself. If he could, he would not need Jesus Christ.

Nor can man change himself. If he could, there would be no need for the Holy Spirit. But it is precisely for this reason that Jesus taught the apostles about the Holy Spirit.

He Himself was going away (John 14:19). He will not remain forever in the flesh. But the Spirit of God can be with them, and He will live in them (John 14:17).

This teaching on the Holy Spirit is unique to the Christian faith. No other religion in the world has any parallel to it. Nor can man himself have "invented" such a teaching.

Perhaps this is the reason why so many Christians are fuzzy about the Holy Spirit. They cannot comprehend what seems to be the rather direct and plain teaching of Jesus.

The Gospel of John opens with the double assertion that Jesus came to take away our sins and to baptize us with the Holy Spirit (John 1:29,34). He who came to die for our sin, came also to impart to us power over sin. He who brings us salvation through the cross also offers us dynamic power through God's Spirit. What Jesus has done *for* us the Holy Spirit will do *in* us.

The mystery will lift like early morning fog if we can begin to believe the words of Jesus and experience the presence of God for ourselves! Let the very uniqueness of Jesus' promise excite us in exploring the possibility, the truth and the dynamic for our lives.

To Go Further

What are you to do? (John 14:23)
How can you show your faith? (John 14:24)
Can you begin to believe the promise?

2nd Day   The Power
Acts 1:1-8

Some people seem to have spiritual power; others lack it. Why? Is this because some have certain virtues and others are defective? No. The difference lies rather in the way some seek first the kingdom of God, while other Christians do not give it too much thought. Some are earnest and persistent. Others have become lazy and careless.

Spiritual power is the most important kind of power. Why are we so slow to see this? Why are we so lax to do something about it?

In a report entitled "Towards the Conversion of England" was the statement: "The church is at present itself a field for evangelism rather than a force for evangelism." And also: "A large proportion of worshipers are only half-converted."

Wouldn't you think that our primary concern ought to be for the awakening of the church? For a renewal within all Christians? For an emphasis on the power of God which is available through the Holy Spirit?

As we have discovered already, at the beginning of Jesus' ministry the emphasis was on the death of Jesus for the sin of the world and His coming to baptize us in the power of the Spirit (John 1:29,34). Having accomplished His work on the cross, the risen Christ spoke of the baptism of the Spirit (Acts 1:5). His promise was one of power (Acts 1:8).

Immediately after making this promise, Jesus ascended to the Father (Acts 1:9-11). He went away in order to clear the way for the coming of the Spirit.

If we believe in the Christ who died for us on the cross, let us even more have faith in His promise of power for living.

To Go Further

Stop criticizing others. Start looking at your own need, your own want of power.

Pray in faith. Believe the promise in Acts 1:8.

It's hardly possible to approach the gift of the Holy Spirit in a theoretical way. Nor can we be analytical about it.

The day of Pentecost was originally a Hebrew feast day (Acts 2:1). It came fifty days after the Passover season, and the word "Pentecost" means fifty.

But this particular Pentecost day was to be a most unusual event. The promise of power which Jesus had made was fulfilled on the apostles, who had gathered together in one place. The account speaks of wind and fire (Acts 2:2,3), which are both symbols of power. Wind can reach hurricane proportions and fire can be devastating in its destruction. And yet wind can blow away the rain, and fire under control can melt steel.

The other symbol of the Spirit is the speaking in tongues (Acts 2:4). But it is clear from this account that this speaking in tongues meant the phenomenon of speaking other languages (Acts 1:6,8). The message was brought by the Spirit through these responsive disciples.

What would happen to us if the Spirit were to descend in power? Could we take it? Would we make objections? Would we demand that the revival adhere to our specifications? Would we insist that the awakening not get out of control or over-emotional?

If we have only been a little bit civilized by our Christianity, we may tend to shy away from the real thing. Not that the Holy Spirit allows things to get out of control. But the Holy Spirit comes in His own way, on His own terms, in the power of God.

Pentecost, as a historical event, will not be repeated. But the Spirit who came can come now, can fall again in power on His church!

To Go Further

What could be happening in your life that is not happening now?

What can you do about it? Specifically?

4th Day   **The Prophecy**
Acts 2:14-21

What we have potentially in the church of Jesus Christ is tremendous. What we are doing with what we have is almost disgusting. Instead of barrelling down the turnpikes and the freeways in a high-powered machine, we are attempting it with a broken-down model T.

New power is available. We are simply not using it, or rather, hooking into it. Our power lines are down, and as a result most denominations are declining in their membership. Sanctuaries are not full, and even Sunday Schools continue to lose ground. All this in the face of a rising population.

When the church begins to see its sickness, it may then reach out for healing. When Christians know their lack of power, they will then begin to pray for awakening. And the time has come when no other business, no more committees, no routine-as-usual should obscure from us the urgency of spiritual renewal.

The impact which the apostles made on the day of Pentecost corresponded to the tumult of a bunch of rowdy drunks (Acts 2:15). But they were not filled with wine. They were filled with the Spirit of God (Ephesians 5:18). Genuine power. Genuine joy. Genuine enthusiasm.

The prophecy of Joel was literally fulfilled (Acts 2:16). All of this was to precede the great day of the Lord (Acts 2:20). And since that day of judgment has not yet come, we are still in the day of the Spirit. His power can fall on us, so that "whosoever shall call on the name of the Lord shall be saved" (Acts 2:21).

This is project #1 for all Christians—the unrestrained, unhindered, controlling presence of the Holy Spirit in our lives—to allow the power of God to fall upon and live through His people.

Let it be project #1 for you!

To Go Further

What is the meaning of Acts 2:17,18?

What will be the outcome of power in our lives? (Acts 2:21)

How can you make it project #1 today?

The apostles were given spiritual power after they had been with Jesus for three years. During that period they learned, they absorbed, they studied, they worked, and they came to know God through Jesus Christ.

The more they were grounded in both experience and knowledge, the more ready they were for the filling of the Spirit.

God does not operate in a vacuum. As we spend more time with Christ in the study of His Word and prayer, we grow in knowledge. As we put into practice what we believe, we grow in practical experience. In this way we become more open to the power of the Holy Spirit, and we will be used as His channels in the world.

There is no quick, easy formula for "spiritual success." God does not entrust Himself to the lazy, the indifferent, or the casual Christians. Only those who believed in Him, who followed Him when He had nowhere to lay His head, and were willing to take up their cross daily, experienced the inrush of power.

And in the hours of persecution which were sure to follow their bold declaration of the gospel, they expressed their essential loyalty to Jesus Christ (Acts 4:12). He was their crucified Saviour, their risen Lord, and the One who was present with them through His Spirit (Acts 4:10,13).

Here, then, is the secret of power. It is in a Person. The living God who has come to earth in the person of His Son is now present in His Spirit. And they who had been with Him during His ministry were now being used by Him as channels of the Spirit.

Without spiritual power we have only the wisdom of man. With the power of God, all things are possible. The more you are grounded in both experience and knowledge, the more ready you are for God's Spirit in your life!

To Go Further

Are you willing to endure opposition?

Do you put Christ central in your life and witness? (Acts 4:10-12)

How can people know you have been with Jesus? (Acts 4:13)

6th Day   **In Practice**
Romans 8:9-17

Let's be practical.

That man or woman whose life is easily engulfed by passion, where a wave of lustful temptation can wash him out to sea, *must* be given power if he or she is to learn control.

That businessman in the sharp competition of this world, who can constantly be molded like putty to practice unacceptable tactics, *must* be given power to enable him to want to be led by his Lord.

9

Any husband or wife (and children too) can so easily let go within the walls of the home, showing a bad temper, a mean disposition, kicking a chair, slamming a door, throwing things. It takes divine power to be gracious and kind, patient and understanding, compassionate yet firm, cheery and tender.

It takes power to keep the body under control, the mind clean and wholesome, the imagination pure, the spirit willing. And the flesh? Yes, the flesh. . . .

That's what the power of God is for, in daily living, in practice. Either flesh or Spirit (Romans 8:8). You are either controlled by your own lusts, or by the Spirit's power (Romans 8:9).

If you believe in Christ, you have also received His Holy Spirit (Romans 8:14). Then begin to live appropriating the power He has promised you (Romans 8:11).

The result of living after the flesh is death (Romans 8:13). The result of living in the Spirit leads to life and to an inheritance in Christ (Romans 8:15-17).

What Scripture teaches is true—in theory.

Let God work it out as well—in practice!

To Go Further

Are you able to say "Father" without fear? (Romans 8:15)

What areas of your life need to be opened to the Holy Spirit today?

Have you ever used a bucket to water some flowers? It's a tiresome exercise. Fill the bucket, carry it to the flower bed, empty the bucket, carry it back to the faucet, and repeat the process over and over.

How much better when there is a hose attached to the faucet and the flow of water is constant. No dry spells, no non-productive time. Just a continuous flow of water to the dry flower bed.

Isn't it exciting to watch a person who has learned the secret of abiding in Christ? His ordinary attitudes and beliefs become great convictions. He moves beyond himself in dedication and service. The love of God fills him and he can't keep from spilling out some of that love.

Some Christians are like buckets. They have come to the giver of living water all right. But they are trying to live on stored-up "water." They do not realize that the Holy Spirit will constantly fill their lives. He will "be in [them] a well of water springing up into everlasting life" (John 4:14).

There is nothing as sad as seeing people who are enjoying their faith as though they had enough of it, and don't expect ever again to be filled to overflowing!

Not so among that early Christian community. After the initial outpouring of the Holy Spirit on Pentecost, they continued to be in contact with Christ (Acts 4:8,31). And they overflowed in various ways: In preaching (Acts 4:31); in fellow-

11

ship (Acts 4:32); in sharing (Acts 4:32-37).

They were concerned for one another. They did not take up an offering for the poor and needy once in a while, or stuff a Christmas basket for some family they could think of on such an occasion. They belonged to one another. They shared their belongings. They felt close enough to carry one another's burdens.

All that came through the Holy Spirit in their lives, the divine Persuader who changed them, empowered them, and filled them to overflowing. He will do the same for us!

To Go Further

Consider the implications of the early church's experiment of sharing. (Acts 4:32-37)

Are you willing to be filled with the Spirit?

Does this mean you will let Him have control?

Make a Decision

The first thing that must happen is between you and Christ. You will never have spiritual power unless you surrender yourself to Him in concrete, specific terms.

Then, drop the old, negative pictures of yourself. Don't say that you can't do anything, that you are unworthy, that you have no "talent." Let Him take over!

Finally, commit yourself to grow in experience

and knowledge, to be willing to serve and give, and to be constantly open to the filling of God's Spirit.

"I know no human being with spiritual power," says Sam Shoemaker, "who did not at some point have to let go of as much as he or she saw, in as complete a surrender as possible."

CHAPTER 2

The Secret of Awakening

It may be necessary for a person to receive a blood transfusion—sometimes. But unless the body can make its own blood, he cannot continue to live. Certainly no one can remain healthy on continual blood transfusions.

An evangelistic campaign, a missionary emphasis week, a special series of preaching are like blood transfusions for the body of Christ. They are necessary when the body is sick, but if the body is healthy it should be producing its own missionary concerns and evangelistic witness.

The early Christians did not need transfusions. They were living in the dynamic of the Spirit of God.

Introductory Bible reading for this week: Acts 2:43–6:7

Revival does not begin because a committee thinks it's a good idea. Nor does it get off the ground because a few people decide to have an evangelistic campaign.

Revival only begins when some individual is revived, when someone is awakened to the depth of his being by the living God. Like D. L. Moody promising in a high moment to be the man God could fully control and use. And, again like Moody, such a person may have had a long exposure to the Christian faith before that moment of awakening.

But then these truths become that person's own. They are realized as *personal* truths. And all that can only take place through genuine contact with the Spirit of God.

Paul pleads for this in his letter to Corinth. These Christians had made of that communion hour a time for feasting and festivities (I Corinthians 11:20-22). They had obscured the need for quiet in the presence of God, for meditation on the cross of Christ, for openness to the Spirit of God.

As a result there were divisions and heresies (I Corinthians 11:18,19). But those who draw near to Christ also draw near to one another. There is no division in Christ (I Corinthians 1:13). Nor is there any heresy, but only truth (John 14:6).

You can never give away what you do not have. You will not have anything until you give time and priority to the gospel. Then Christ and the Spirit of Christ will possess you, and you will be able to give away that which has possession of you.

No, renewal will never take place in the church through committees or meetings. It can only happen when you begin to pray: "Lord, revive Thy church, beginning with me."

To Go Further

Can you pray that prayer honestly?

Are you willing to take time in communion with Christ?

Are you willing to take action against the divisions in your church and fellowship?

2nd Day   The Secret of Growth
Ephesians 4:11-16

A seminary student was wrestling with the question of awakening. He was challenged by the need to go beyond the academic and the theological. But the question with which he had to wrestle was simply: "Would I let Jesus Christ become the dominant factor in my life, or wouldn't I?"

He knew many facts. He was not so ready to surrender. Finally, after five hours of discussion, he knelt in prayer and surrendered himself as fully as he could. And something happened.

"I hope that I never get any higher than I was kneeling on that floor," he said. That's where the Christian revolution begins.

Revival does not take great saints. Or else there would seldom be a revival. It only takes willing men and women, who are ready to make the surrender of their lives in simple faith.

This is part of that growth of which Paul writes to the Ephesians. We are to grow up into Christ (Ephesians 4:15). We are no longer to remain children, but learn to commit ourselves in maturity of faith (Ephesians 4:14). The result will be that we speak the truth in love (Ephesians 4:15).

"It is easier to serve God without a vision, easier to work for God without a call, because then you are not bothered by what God requires," writes Oswald Chambers. But the moment you concern yourself with what God requires, the moment you begin to search the Scriptures in earnest, the moment you take seriously the work of the Holy Spirit, you are on your way toward that awakening without which the church will simply fade away more and more.

It is not a matter of time, but of intensity. You do not have to agonize hours on end, but you must be in earnest.

To Go Further

What growth is taking place in your life?

Do you speak the truth in love?

How, specifically, should you be growing up into *Christ*?

3rd Day The Secret of the Spirit
I Corinthians 12:4-11

One reason why we can't seem to have the revival we often talk about is that self gets in the way. We expect to do the job for God. We will give our best to the Master. We will work till the night comes.

We have already become aware of the fact that God will not impart His Spirit to the lazy, and this is not to encourage sloth and unconcern. But awakening is not a matter of self-effort, rather Spirit-effort. God works in and through us. We do not work *for* God.

We can only put ourselves at His disposal. We can only become channels which He can use. A wire does not need to suck the power from the dynamo. It needs only to be brought in touch with that dynamo. It may surprise us when we stop trying to do jobs for God, and simply offer ourselves to be used by His Spirit.

That is the secret of the Holy Spirit. If we could do it on our own, we would not be in need of the Spirit of God. But since we need the Spirit of God, we *can't* do it on our own.

Through the Spirit of God we make our initial confession of Christ (I Corinthians 12:3). Through the Spirit of God the various gifts are given to the church (I Corinthians 12:8-10). And all this takes place under the sovereignty of the Holy Spirit: "As he will" (I Corinthians 12:11). Not, as *I* will.

Our own efforts may stand in His way as much as our other sins.

We need to pray and be open to the working of God's Spirit, and *then* carry out what He leads us to do. We are not masters, but servants. We are not creators, but carriers of the truth. We are not originators, but channels of power.

To Go Further

Are there areas in your life which you don't want to yield to the Spirit? Why not?

Do you condemn in others what you allow in yourself?

Are you willing to become a channel?

4th Day The Secret of Prayer
Acts 5:12-26

When once the Lord takes hold of you, it is likely that He will bring you in touch with other concerned Christians. You will become part of a group in which you can be honest, speak of your needs, pray about your concerns, and begin to explore areas of service.

It may not be the same old group that already exists in the church. It may become a fresh new group which is brought together by that same Spirit of God.

Jesus brought a group of twelve together, and they changed the world. Part of their secret lay in the power of prayer.

The early Christian community was a community of faith. There were many signs and wonders wrought through their fellowship (Acts 5:12). And when persecution struck, they prayed together for deliverance (Acts 12:5). As a result deliverance came and Peter was released from prison (Acts 5:19).

It would not have been possible to bring about the witness recorded in Acts 5:28, except for the power of the Holy Spirit working mightily through that dedicated fellowship. The group was vital to them, the group which prayed together and grew in the Lord.

If enough individuals will band together in the power of the Spirit to pray and seek God, we may get a converted church, a revived church, an awakened church. Only an awakened church can be used in a hostile world.

The power is available. Jesus has promised it. The Holy Spirit has already come into the world, and He is with us until the very end. He needs only our willingness.

The secret of awakening is in communion, growth, prayer and the Holy Spirit of God.

To Go Further

Read carefully the passage for today, and the parallel in Acts 12:1-18.

Is prayer a reality to you? How can it become so now?

Someone has said that the ordinary Christian's blood pressure is so low that when it reaches normal, he thinks he has a fever.

Pentecost is normal Christianity! Anything else is subnormal. We have become so used to the anemic, matter-of-fact, ordinary fellowship which we have, that the fire and excitement and stir of the early Christians is hardly seen among us. But when we read the book of the Acts, we are convinced that the Christianity described in it is normal and ours is below average.

We are too easily satisfied with a cultural hangover, with second best and with a watered-down version of the real thing. When we daily get in touch with God, He will use us to change our own and other people's lives. We will then approach what He has actually intended for us.

The secret of that awakening is in Christ. The early Christians knew that the mystery which had been hidden in previous times was now made known to them (Colossians 1:26). What was this mystery, this previously hidden secret? "Christ in you, the hope of glory" (Colossians 1:27). This is the power that works within the "normal" Christian (Colossians 1:29).

It was a totally new concept. No one had ever talked about Moses or a prophet living within them, but the Christians freely confessed that the power within them was Christ. He had promised to be with them even unto the end of the age (Matthew 28:20). They said, "He is alive forevermore, risen from the dead. He is the living Lord" (Philippians 2:11).

Here, then, is the new dynamic for Christian living. The power is not of man, but of God. The dynamic is not human but divine. The source is not in man but in Christ.

To Go Further

To what extent will this mean suffering? (Colossians 1:24) What kind of "suffering"?

Is Christ living in you?

What should be some of the evidence? (Colossians 1:28,29)

6th Day **In Love**
Colossians 3:12-17

Her husband lay ill. She had been married to him for nearly fifty years. She said to the minister when he called: "We've had a lot of years together and we're still hopelessly in love with each other."

That kind of devotion is not common. Those who are hopelessly in love are usually found in the engagement period, or perhaps the early months of marriage. But few husbands or wives would say they are hopelessly in love with each other. And yet . . . ?

To what extent is this a parallel to our Christian experience? When we first became Christians there was this early glow, this beginning zeal. Are we "still hopelessly in love"? What happened? Is it difficult to maintain that glow?

Consider the faithfulness of the Lord. Our problem lies not in Him but in our faithlessness. Our hope is in God. When we look to Him, our love for Him and for our fellowman will increase. As we meditate upon His love for us our times of quietness and prayer will become more meaningful. When our lives are filled with Christ we will find that we are "still hopelessly in love."

Consider what should be added in the Christian life (Colossians 3:12). There should be a deep personal relationship among Christians in forgiveness and respect (Colossians 3:13). Above all, love ought to characterize our fellowship (Colossians 3:14).

All this becomes possible as the peace of God acts as an umpire in our hearts (Colossians 3:15), and the word of God lives in us richly (Colossians 3:16).

The secret of awakening is not only in our relationship to God, but also in our ability to live in peace and forgiveness with one another. When the Spirit of God floods our lives, what this passage speaks about will be a reality.

Above all love (charity in the K.J.V.) which is the bond of perfection (Colossians 3:14).

To Go Further

Pray for these qualities to be in you.
Are you forgiving? Will you forgive—everyone?

24

Are you kind, merciful, patient?
Does God's peace rule in your life?

7th Day   In Faith
Hebrews 11:32–12:2

Is it too much to expect that every Christian who knows who Jesus Christ is and has been converted through faith to:

1. Be able to share that faith in simple words?
2. Keep up the habit of personal devotion and meditation?
3. Rely on the Holy Spirit for power and wisdom?
4. Become a channel of God's Spirit, radiating His peace and power?

That is normal Christianity. That is New Testament Christianity. And the way to revival is in communion, in prayer, in love, in faith, *in Christ!*

"Looking unto Jesus the author and finisher of our faith" (Hebrews 12:2). He is the originator and the perfecter of faith. He is the only one who can give us the faith we need to please God. The great heroes listed earlier in the passage are important, but faith is a gift of God through Jesus Christ. The others in Hebrews 11 were men and women who "hooked into" the power of God—by faith. You cannot read the chapter without the realization that the secret of their godly lives lay in their faith in God.

They won great victories by faith (Hebrews 11:32-35). They also went down to bitter defeats (Hebrews 11:36-69). In spite of the loss of life and limb, of earthly possessions and all things, they obtained a good report. No matter what happened to them on earth, they continued to believe in God, and they believed utterly!

Let this example encourage us. They witness to us (Hebrews 12:1). For the secret of awakening lies in the reality of faith, in daily living by that certainty that "if God be for us, who can be against us" (Romans 8:31)?

By faith.

To Go Further

Compare the successes and the failures of faith. (Hebrews 11:32-38)

How is Jesus the originator of faith? The perfecter of your faith?

Make a Decision

A college girl sat down in the cafeteria and bowed her head in prayer. Her five companions snickered.

"What were you laughing at?" she asked.

"You know."

"Aren't you grateful?" she asked.

"For what?"

"The food."

"Why? We bought it."

"Where'd you get the money?"

"Family," they said.

"Where'd they get it?"

"Worked for it," they replied.

"Where'd they get the power to work?"

She pushed it all back to God. That night when they ate together again, two others prayed. The next day all of them said grace.

How can you share your faith? *Today*?

CHAPTER 3

Open the Door
and Get Out of the Doorway

"Sir, do you remember when you were at Prudhoe two years ago?" asked a woman of John Wesley. "You breakfasted at Thomas Newton's. I am his sister. You looked upon me as you were going out and said, 'Be in earnest.' I knew not then what earnestness meant, nor had I any thought about it; but the words sank into my heart, so that I could never rest anymore, till I sought and found Christ."

God is able to use you, even you, when you share the good news. It's not so difficult. Use simply words. Open the door that others may enter in. Open the door and get out of the doorway.

Introductory Bible reading for this week: Galatians 3

1st Day   Of Man or God?
Galatians 1:6-12

You can substitute a chair for a chair, but you cannot substitute a table for a chair. Even chairs which are different can replace one another, but a table is in a different class.

There is no alternative for the gospel of God. There is nothing of the same kind, or in the same class (Galatians 1:8,9). Why?

Because this is the good news of revelation. It is not of man but of God. It is not human but divine. It is not given with the approval of man, but as the direct light from above (Galatians 1:11,12). It is not attained but obtained, not aspired after but received.

This is the uniqueness of the Christian gospel. When you are convinced of this truth, you cannot help but share it in all its simplicity. You see this conviction in Paul's writing and in his life. He knew there could be no substitute for this revealed word.

Why do we attempt to make religion out of the gospel? Why do we reduce the gospel to theology and talk, to formal or informal worship, to second-hand sentiments which we receive from others, to clichés that go no deeper than the human mind?

The New Testament presents a direct encounter with God, a revelation which came from the living Christ, a transformation which took place in the hearts of the early Christians, a Word that reached into lives and had its impact on the surrounding world.

This is the good news. Unadulterated, pure, vital, vibrant—and it shook the world, once. When we receive it in its essence, the gospel can do in us and through us what it did then.

Neither the gospel nor the Holy Spirit has changed. The dilution is in us.

To Go Further

What was the problem in Galatia? (1:6,7)
Do similar problems exist today?
How can you be a servant of Christ? (1:10)

2nd Day   Of Works or Faith?
Galatians 3:6-14

If the gospel is revelation from God, it can only be received by faith. Man cannot work for it. Man cannot qualify for it. It must be given from above.

Man can only live by faith, as Abraham did (Galatians 3:6). And since Abraham was the friend of God not because of his accomplishments but because he took God at His word, we are the children of Abraham when we walk in faith (Galatians 3:7). In fact, this is how the nations will come to the light (Galatians 3:8). By faith.

Faith means a constancy of purpose, a confidence in the living God, a reliance in trust. The

Hebrew word for faith means to strengthen, to support, to hold up as you would support a baby in your arms. The Greek word for faith is the opposite of mistrust and reaches even into the area of persuasion. To believe is to be persuaded, to rely utterly on the object of your faith.

Not in faith itself, but in its object. Not faith in faith, but faith in Christ. Not faith in prayer, but faith in the Holy Spirit.

When you face Jesus directly, He is likely to ask you whether you believe. He constantly encouraged the people that came to Him (in the Gospels) to express their faith in action. And in His presence you begin to feel that faith is as natural as breathing. You may even be surprised why it was so difficult to trust Him before.

If you are not living in touch with Him, it is easy to drift away from faith. The secret lies in that relationship. "The just shall live by faith" (Galatians 3:11).

Not merely become Christians, but *live*.

Faith that is sure of itself is hardly faith. But faith that is sure of God is faith indeed.

To Go Further

Compare works and faith. (Galatians 3:10-12)
Are you living by faith? How can you be?
Express your thanksgiving for the redemption in Christ! (Galatians 3:13,14)

32

If the gospel comes to us from God and is received by faith, man cannot qualify by keeping certain laws and regulations.

"You've taken the Ten Commandments from us," said a Jew.

"But we haven't kept them either," answered the Christian.

Why, then, did God give the Law to man? It was a temporary measure (Galatians 3:19). But it was obvious that the Law could not solve the problem of sin. Man soon came to learn this in his long history of failure. If the Law could have given life, then it would not have been necessary for Christ to come and die. The Law would have been an easier method of achieving salvation (Galatians 3:21).

So the Law was temporary and preparatory, like school. For educational and moral purposes until school is out, until we reach maturity (Galatians 3:24,25).

Often the education of those times was the responsibility of a schoolmaster, who came between the parent and the child. Paul refers to such a schoolmaster, but when the task has been completed, he steps out of the way and the parent and child are brought together again.

We are the children of God by faith in Jesus Christ (Galatians 3:26). School's out. Grow up in faith. Live in that new relationship of grace.

Grasp the scope of this good news! Receive the unique revelation which has been given us in Jesus

Christ! Enter into that awakening which the Spirit
wants to bring about in the church! Open the door
of your life to Him, and you will be opening the
door for others—soon.

To Go Further

If you have become a Christian, have you *put on
Christ?* (Galatians 3:27)
How can you do this? What ought you to do?
What difference will it make? (Galatians 3:28)

4th Day   **For Jew or All?**
Acts 10:34-43

Don't ever think that the early Christians were
without problems. One of the most serious was the
prejudice which ran deep among the Jewish believers. It was simply inconceivable to them that the
Gentiles should be included in the gospel. They
stuck only to the evangelizing of the Jews.

In spite of what Jesus had said to them (Acts
1:8)! Only a few, like Philip, ventured beyond the
established boundaries (Acts 8:5). Peter even ar-
gued with the Lord about it (Acts 10:14). He had
been accorded a special vision, but he was reluc-
tant to accept the message (Acts 10:11-17).

But the Holy Spirit was able to move Peter into
new adventures. He went with the men who had

come from Cornelius, a Roman officer in the Roman army. At the beginning of his speech to Cornelius he revealed his prejudice (Acts 10:34,35). By the grace of God he overcame it.

The message which the early Christians preached centered in Jesus Christ as the Lord of all (Acts 10:36). He was anointed of God (Acts 10:38). In His earthly ministry He went about doing good (Acts 10:38,39). He was crucified and raised from the dead (Acts 10:39,40). He is the Judge of all (Acts 10:42). It is a matter of responding by faith for the forgiveness of sins (Acts 10:43).

In Christ there is no room for prejudice. Plato gives thanks that he is a man and not an animal, a Greek and not a barbarian, a man and not a woman. But in Christ all national, social, physical, economic and racial distinctions pass away. "Ye are all one in Christ" (Galatians 3:28).

By the power of the Spirit our prejudices can be overcome. By the power of the Spirit the church can be rejuvenated. Old things will fade away and all things can become new.

The time for awakening is *now*.

To Go Further

Do you have any prejudice to overcome?

How can you be changed, even now?

Does the message Peter preached have any effect on you? (Acts 10:36-43)

"I am debtor" (Romans 1:14). That doesn't
sound strange coming from Paul, now that you
know how deeply grateful he was for the gospel
which had been revealed to him, and the Christ
who had been revealed *in* him.

He felt his indebtedness to the whole world (Romans 1:14). He included rich and poor, wise and
unwise, slave and free—all men. His indebtedness
was the result of the grace which he had experienced, and therefore he was ready to witness to
this good news everywhere (Romans 1:15).

He had experienced it as the power unto salvation, first for himself, then as it was proclaimed
(Romans 1:16). He was certain that the way of
faith is the only way to live (Romans 1:17).

The indebtedness of Paul was not a burden for
him; it was a joy to share. It was not a hardship,
but a privilege.

There is a story about the late Lord Halifax who
was a very devout Christian. He was listening to
two leading bishops of the Church of England discussing the social welfare of Great Britain, and of
the need for more social justice.

Suddenly Lord Halifax interrupted: "I can't
think how you can be so interested in what happens in a world which is about to be burned up
sooner or later."

In spite of that fact, it is a world into which the
Son of God came to die for the sin of man. It is a
world into which the early Christians went with a

great indebtedness to proclaim the good news of salvation. And it is a world which is desperately sick in our time, sick and in need, lost and faltering on the brink of disaster.

We are debtors of the grace of God to bring the good news of God. But only the very few accept this responsibility. Until the entire church wakes up, we will merely drift along with the tides to nowhere. . . .

To Go Further

Consider your indebtedness to God.
Pray about your indebtedness to man.
Ask Him to lead you to someone, today.

6th Day   When God Shows You
Acts 10:24-29

A national came to a Christian missionary and said: "We found you out, sir. You are not as good as your Book."

What would he say to the Christians at home?

No, we are not as good as our Book. We do not pretend to be perfect. But we are to be people of the Book. We are to be ambassadors for Christ, *worthy* representatives (II Corinthians 5:20). What of our *holy* calling in Christ (II Timothy 1:9)?

We have already discovered that Peter was

37

changed by the vision accorded him from God. He spoke freely of his earlier prejudices to Cornelius, and confessed that God changed his mind (Acts 10:28,29).

When God shows you, are you willing to listen? When God shows you, are you willing to change? When God shows you, will you step out to become a witness?

A witness is a person who tells what he has seen and heard. Take any person on the witness stand in a court room. If he begins to talk about things he cannot verify, he is quickly stopped. He can only speak of that which is outside the realm of hearsay.

So you must deepen your experience of Christ and your knowledge of the gospel. As you grow in knowledge and experience, you will become an effective spokesman for God.

A witness is a person whose faith and life are one. When the challenge comes to testify, a witness will do so "disregarding all risks, accepting all consequences," writes Whittaker Chambers in his book *Witness*.

When God shows you. . . . What has God shown you recently, today?

To Go Further

Ask God to show you what He wants from you!
Pray about an awakening in your life.
"Are you as good as your Book?" What can you do about it?

He was at the end of his rope. Should he continue his musical ambitions? Should he call it quits?
One day alone in his apartment—almost in desper-
ation—he grabbed at a piece of music and started
to sing it. It was the Lord's Prayer. His courage returned and he sang it again in full voice.

A few days later a note was slipped under his
door. "Dear Neighbor: If ever you feel discour-
aged, perhaps this will hearten you," it read.

"Things had been going badly for me—so badly
I didn't want to live any longer. When I'd hear you
practicing I'd snap out of it a little, because you
sounded as though you had something to live for.
But the other night I decided to end my life. I
went into the kitchen and turned on the gas. Then
I heard you singing the Lord's Prayer. Suddenly I
realized what I was doing. I turned off the gas,
opened the windows and drank in the fresh air."

There was a conclusion: "Well, you saved my
life. You gave me the courage to make a decision I
should have made long ago. Now life is all I could
hope it to be. Thanks always."

We will never *know* how many lives we have affected for good or ill. But we can put ourselves at
God's disposal, and the Holy Spirit can use us as
His channels in a world of need. We can pray for
God's mercy upon us and all our ways (Psalm
67:1). We can pray that His way may be known
among all nations (Psalm 67:2).

The Scriptural view is not merely individual. It

is national. It is for the world. The ends of the earth are to hear the good news (Psalm 67:4,7).

So, open the door and step out of the doorway.

To Go Further

What is the purpose of proclamation? (Psalm 67:3)

What is the meaning of praise? How do you praise God?

Pray to be used as a channel of the Spirit.

Make a Decision

A Christian called on one family for over five years. They never did respond. Finally, he decided to throw their card away, but before he did so, he made one last effort. As a result of that call, they came to church and later accepted Christ.

What if he had given up? One pastor says that a prospect on his list is never removed unless he dies or moves away.

What does it mean to be a witness? Are you willing to persist? Is there someone on whom you have all but given up?

Be specific in your response and decision.

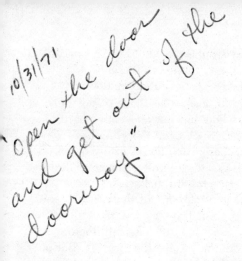

10/31/71

'open the door
and get out of the
doorway.'

CHAPTER 4

The Dynamics of Explosion

"It may be," says Dibelius, "that the church of Jesus Christ has but the same task as the chaplain in a prison where those condemned to death are kept; to prepare mankind for its end."

Although we have never been commissioned to convert the world, we have been commissioned to evangelize, to create the atmosphere of choice, to bring the good news so that men may crown Him or crucify Him, to challenge them to prepare for the coming judgment.

As the early church exploded beyond the walls of Jerusalem, so the twentieth century church needs to explode with this good news.

Introductory Bible reading for this week: Acts 6:8–8:40; 10:1–11:18

The story of the early Christians is not only a story of joyous fellowship but of creative hardship. The persecutions swept over the church as wave follows wave to shore, each one crashing down (so it seemed) with greater intensity, but never breaking the back of these faithful believers.

The waves of persecution had the effect of scattering the Christians. They moved from place to place, until it became too difficult, until the opposition was too hostile to receive the message. But out of their troubles the blessing was passed on to others, and people heard the good news who would otherwise not have heard it.

This was the effect of the martyrdom of Stephen, the first Christian to give his life for the cause of Christ (Acts 7:59). As a result the Christians went everywhere (Acts 8:1).

"Except the apostles" (Acts 8:1)! That's an arresting note. They were the trained, the ones who had been with Jesus. They were the original followers, and they stayed behind in Jerusalem.

That means those young Christians, those newer ones, went elsewhere with the good news. The parallel might be that the trained preachers remained in the churches, while the membership went everywhere proclaiming the good news.

The church exists for the world! It does not exist for itself. In fact, the church is the only organization in the world that does not exist for its members.

The minister is God's gift to the church. The church is God's gift to the world. That is how the early church exploded—*through its membership,* not through the clergy.

Some encouraging lay movements are taking place in our time. But the greatest movement is that which the Holy Spirit can generate in His church as we are willing and obedient.

To Go Further

Does trouble make you close up, or does it lead you into new adventures for Christ? Why?

Can you be this forgiving? (Acts 7:60)

Are you willing to listen to the Word of God today?

2nd Day   **To the North**
Acts 8:4-8

A young Christian was standing in front of a downtown mission in Chicago. He was giving out tracts. A man who was quite inebriated attempted to draw a knife on him. The student with his wits about him said:

"I have something sharper than you have. Let me show you."

The man stopped and stared. The student pulled out his Bible and read: "The word of God is quick, and powerful, and sharper than any two-edged

43

sword" (Hebrews 4:12). Quietly and submissively the man entered the mission.

Not everyone can be as sharp as that. How often have you driven home after an important conversation and said to yourself, "Why didn't I think of that? Why didn't I say that?"

But do you ever look back on a conversation and see how the Spirit of God did work through you? He will lead you in what you are to say. You need only be open to Him. You can rely on the promise of Matthew 10:19,20.

So they went everywhere preaching the Word (Acts 8:4). That Word is equated with Christ (Acts 8:5). *He* is that Word. The early Christians did not have a Bible. They had only that event to proclaim, that God was in Christ and that in Him forgiveness of sins is a possibility for all who believe. They had only the cross, the resurrection and His return to judge the world to announce. So the Word they preached was Christ (John 1:1,14; Acts 8:4,5).

The Samaritans to whom Philip went were not on the best terms with the Jews (Acts 8:5). Again these Christians overcame their prejudice as they announced the good news to non-Jews. And the result was great joy in that city (Acts 8:8)!

To Go Further

What is the good news you share?
Are you willing to overcome your prejudices?
Consider John 4:9 in connection with Acts 8:5.

But Samaria wasn't all. The man who had overcome his prejudices by going to the Samaritans was
again used by God in a new venture. This time he
did not go into a city, but into a desert (Acts 8:26).
This time not to many people, but only to one man
(Acts 8:27). This time not to those who were part-
ly Jews, as were the Samaritans, but to a man from
another continent and another color.

A man of great influence; a man with spiritual
hunger; a man who was searching the Scriptures
(Acts 8:28).

Philip felt led to approach him, and he did it
with a simple, direct question (Acts 8:30). Not
very theological. Not very profound. Not very unusual. But the question was enough to reach the
mark (Acts 8:31).

As they rode on together Philip began at the
very place to preach (proclaim) Jesus, just as he
had done in Samaria (Acts 8:5,35). The proclamation led up to an understanding and a desire to follow Christ. The Ethiopian asked about baptism
(Acts 8:36).

Now comes the direct approach—"if thou believ-
est" (Acts 8:37)! The man made a simple confession of faith and was baptized (Acts 8:38).

Philip's mission was completed. He was sent in
another direction, as the man from Ethiopia went
on his way rejoicing in Christ (Acts 8:39). Philip
left the city of Samaria as well as the Ethiopian
eunuch rejoicing (Acts 8:8,39).

It is not hard to witness. It begins with simple questions, as we draw out the other person. It leads to direct proclamation. We do not argue or debate, but present Jesus Christ, the Son of God. It ends in confrontation—do you believe?

There is no one way. But whoever is willing to be guided by the Spirit will be used as a channel. One thing is for sure. When a church loses its desire to witness, it loses its right to be called a church!

To Go Further

Will you pray for God's guidance today?
Are you ready to be used by His Spirit?
Let Him remove any fears, any obstruction.

4th Day   **To the East**
Acts 9:19b-22

The gospel is news, not views. Little is gained by argument and disputing. "You must tell men what God says and leave it there," said Spurgeon. God's Word is to be believed, not reasoned about. Religion is not only for the intellect, it makes a demand on faith.

How straightforward is the New Testament as it relates the explosion which occurred in the early church. They all preached Christ. They did not deviate from that message (Acts 9:20,22).

I once heard someone suggest that you can begin your witnessing by asking: "Do you want the world to be a better place for your having lived?"

The obvious answer to that question will be a "yes."

Then: "Do you think the Christian or the non-Christian life is better?"

The answer will probably be: "The Christian. But. . . ."

The next step, said he, is to deal with the "buts."

That's a clever way to get to the main problems of that individual. But ultimately you must get beyond them to the proclamation of Christ. For that, keep going back to the New Testament. Go directly to the words of Jesus. Don't point out merely those things which others said about Him, but show how He Himself proclaimed Himself the Son of God, the Way, the Truth and the Life. The words of Jesus will cause men to make decisions, either for or against Him.

You must have a cause, not just make a case.

Dr. Elton Trueblood says that we must either advance or decay. Any group that ceases to grow and spread is already dying. Standing still is stagnation and sure death.

Let the living Christ work in you by His Spirit in order that the church may come alive.

To Go Further

Read through the always remarkable conversion of Paul in Acts 9:1-20.

47

Are you willing to be put through the paces to be used by the Spirit of God?

5th Day **To the West**
Acts 13:4-12

An old man was fishing. He pulled in one trout after another. The other men working farther downstream were not doing so well. One of them stood by, watching. Finally he asked him his secret.

"Well, there are three rules for trout fishing," said the experienced fisherman. "The first is to keep yourself out of sight. The second is to keep yourself farther out of sight. And the third is to keep yourself completely out of sight."

God does work through persons, but every person needs to keep "out of sight." We should not get in front of the cross, but behind it. We preach Christ crucified and not ourselves (I Corinthians 2:2; II Corinthians 4:5).

The dynamics of explosion are the work of the Spirit of God, not ours (Acts 13:4). He is the starter of missions and witness. And His is the power that flows through men, as the electric power flows through the wires from the plant to our homes (Acts 13:9).

Do you have convictions but not power? Do you hold strong moral beliefs, but lack contagion? Do you belong to committees or fellowships, yet you are not busy transmitting the explosive gospel of Christ?

There is only one answer to this miserable situation. *Repent and believe the good news!* Turn from these ineffective ways, from a lukewarm life, from going around in circles which get you nowhere. Become aware of God, of His presence, His love, His compassion for the lost. Open yourself to the influence of His Spirit. Learn at the feet of Christ through His Word. Know that God has called you into the faith and is *now* doing and working and living.

Those who become aware of God will be used by God. Those who draw near to Christ will believe the good news. Those who are open to the Spirit will be channels of the Spirit.

To Go Further

Be honest about the above questions. Face yourself as you are now. Turn to the living God.

Believe that He can and will use even you!

6th Day   And All the Rest
Matthew 28:16-20

"When Paul said, 'Quit ye like men,' he was not thinking of those Christians who are rocked in the cradle of a conservative church, by the slippered foot of a soft-speaking minister, to all delicate ditties; but of a stalwart soldier, with his face as bronzed as his helmet, and ready for the fray."

Henry Ward Beecher went on to say: "It is not a man's part merely to keep his armor bright; to hang around the edge of the fight, and, whenever he sees it bulging out towards him, to retreat to a hill. . . . It is a man's business to go down to the battle, and to use his sword when he gets there."

There will always be conflict and intimidation. This is why Jesus emphasized that all power belongs to Him in heaven and in earth (Matthew 28:18)! The power is not ours, but His. The power can be ours only through the Holy Spirit (Acts 1:8).

In a world that may often be hostile, the assurance of the power of Christ will lead us to fulfill the great commission (Matthew 28:19). But not only is all power His. His presence is with us, and He will not leave us until the end comes (Matthew 28:20).

This assurance of His presence is fulfilled by the gift of the Holy Spirit. The Spirit is God-with-us-now. The Spirit is the Spirit of Christ. The Spirit is to live within us (Romans 8:11).

We have followed the disciples as they went to the north, the south, the east and the west proclaiming the good news. They went in fulfillment of the call to go into *all the world* (Matthew 28:19). No nation should be excluded from the saving message of Christ.

If God so loved the world that He gave His Son, we need to go into all the world to spread that Word.

To Go Further

Do you really believe Matthew 28:18?

Do you believe Matthew 28:20?

If you cannot be a missionary "out there," are you willing to be used right where you are?

7th Day   His Way Is Best
Romans 11:7-16

He was watching the three little girls standing in front of the store window. It was just before Christmas, and they were looking over the selection of toys. Two of them were trying to tell the third what was in that window.

She was blind. She had never been able to see. And her sisters were describing it all to her. The hardest task of all seemed to be that of picturing the toys for their blind sister.

We are often in that position, too. Men are blind (Romans 11:25). They cannot see the beauty in Christ. They do not recognize their need for Him. They cannot grasp the salvation that has been purchased for them at such a price on the cross.

But the blindness of Israel became an opportunity for the Gentile world (Romans 11:12). The converted apostle Paul had such a deep yearning for the salvation of his own people that he became God's ambassador to the Gentile world (see Acts 26:17,18; Romans 9:1-3).

God knows what He is doing in His world. We

may question His ways, but we know that He has not cast aside His own people. "All Israel shall be saved" (Romans 11:26). The blindness is temporary.

Many questions arose in Paul's own mind as he proclaimed the unsearchable riches of Christ and experienced rejection, rebuff and persecution. But he always came to that resounding conclusion of faith: "O the depth of the riches both of the wisdom and knowledge of God! how unsearchable are his judgments, and his ways past finding out" (Romans 11:33).

The mystery of it all did not keep him from active faith and witness. The Spirit of God wants to use us in our time, for all the world.

To Go Further

Are you willing to move beyond your questions to faith and action?

Pray that He will give you true vision!

Become a channel of His power—today.

Make a Decision

In a discussion one person pleads that Christians should witness to everyone they meet. They should talk to the mailman, the milkman, the cabdriver—everybody.

Another admits this is very hard for him. But he

does share his faith in Christ with those who express themselves to him.

Still another Christian finds it difficult to talk about Christ. But she is always busy helping neighbors, people in need, doing for others.

How do you feel about this? Do they all have a piece of the action? What is the meaning of "witnessing"?

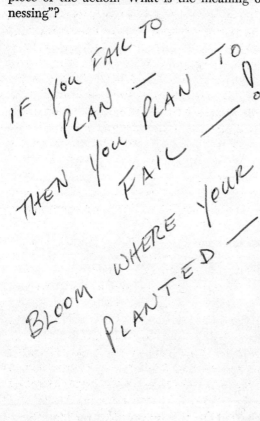

IF you FAIL TO PLAN —

THEN you PLAN TO FAIL — !

BLOOM WHERE your PLANTED —

CHAPTER 5

The Dynamics of Conversion

"This is ridiculous," exclaimed Peppermint Patty who had come to help Charlie Brown and his friends in a consistently losing baseball season. "I've hit five home runs and pitched a no-hit game, and we're behind thirty-seven to five! Whoever heard of thirty-seven unearned runs? I thought I could help your team, but it's hopeless. I'm going back where I came from."

As she left, a disconsolate Charlie Brown mused: "That must be a nice thing to be able to do."

We cannot go back to where we came from, but we can be forgiven. We can experience the grace of God and be converted. And that means we can begin again; we can have a new start!

Introductory Bible reading for this week: Acts 9:1-31; 11:19-30; Galatians 1:11-17

If you ever discuss a vacation trip with a travel agent, he will most likely describe the most exotic, faraway places in appealing, delectable language. But if you should ever ask him whether he has been in all those places, he is likely to say: "Well, I've been to Canada, but I haven't been *there.*"

Isn't it all too easy for us as Christians to be a kind of spiritual travel agency, to advertise all the benefits of Christianity in the most extravagant language. If someone should ask us whether we have experienced it, we are forced to reply: "Well, I haven't been there...."

The New Testament Christians spoke from personal experience. Nothing was hearsay. Nothing was secondhand. Nothing was manufactured. The events on which they based their faith were not fables (II Peter 1:16).

Peter wrote about being an eyewitness of the majesty of Christ (verse 16). He told of hearing the voice from heaven (verse 17). And the most telling words of that personal experience are recorded in verse 18: "We were with him in the holy mount."

God is a God who has revealed Himself. He broke the silence of eternity at the baptism of Jesus and on the mountain of transfiguration. He came into the world in His Son and spoke to us.

There can be no conversion unless we receive the revelation of God in Jesus Christ. And there will be no awakening in the church unless we are "converted Christians." That is primary. That is first.

But just in case you should envy the apostles who were *there*, be sure that you realize we have an even more certain Word of prophecy (verse 19). That is the Word revealed through the Holy Spirit (verse 21). Even though we were not there on the mountain, we have that Word too!

To Go Further

Have you been there? Is your Christianity real? Can you speak with assurance? Why?

Think through the passage, II Peter 1:19-21.

2nd Day Observation
I John 1:1-4

Suppose you were to ask some people the simple question: "What must I do to be saved?" You might get any one of the following answers.

"What must you do to be saved? Let me be honest with you. In view of our current knowledge of the Bible and modern scholarship, I would say that you have asked a meaningless question. Personal salvation is a primitive idea which does not belong in the twentieth century."

Or: "Go to work. Clean up the conditions in the world. Become active. Don't worry so much about your personal salvation, for you will be saved in serving your fellowman."

Or: "You already are saved. God has already saved you. Accept it. Start living that way. There is nothing you have to do, so get involved."

Such answers are far removed from the direct message of repentance and faith, or the simple answer that Paul gave to that very question: "Believe on the Lord Jesus Christ, and thou shalt be saved" (Acts 16:31).

First Peter and then John spoke of a personal experience. "We have heard . . . we have seen . . . we have looked upon . . . our hands have handled" (I John 1:1). That which they observed with their eyes and heard with their ears was the eternal Word (verse 2). The written word bears witness to that Word which was a reality in their lives (verse 4).

Religion must be real, salvation an actual experience. We should not explain it away. We must not intellectualize it. Nor should we make it so mysterious that it is removed from the common man.

You will be converted when you receive the revelation of God in Christ by faith, when you turn from your sins in repentance, when you acknowledge Him as Lord (Romans 10:9,10).

Don't make it so difficult. Even a child can receive the Saviour.

To Go Further

Do you honestly receive John's witness in I John 1:1,2? What does it mean to you today?

Is this fellowship (verse 3) a reality for you? How can it be?

3rd Day **Confrontation**
Acts 9:1-9

Peter recounted the revelation from the holy mount. John wrote of touching and seeing the Word of life. And Paul was confronted on the road to Damascus by the living Christ.

Through these three principal persons the Holy Spirit moved mightily in the early church and the revival spread. Still, basic to that dynamic movement is the reality of the conversion experience, the note of personal discovery of the truth, the certainty of inner revelation. "I have heard of thee by the hearing of the ear: but now mine eye seeth thee" (Job 42:5).

The conversion of Paul has always fascinated us. He was dead set against Christ and the Christians. He would hear none of that "nonsense" about a resurrected Man. He had determined to extinguish this sect of heretics (Acts 9:1,2). And he, of all people, was converted.

Do we appreciate the shock of that experience when Paul raised the question, "Who art thou, Lord" (Acts 9:5)? He did not expect to hear, "I am Jesus." But he could not deny the voice nor disparage the vision. The very one whom he had been persecuting turned out to be the long looked for Messiah. And He was alive!

Paul accepted the confrontation without argument (Acts 9:6). His ready obedience showed his willing spirit. And from that moment on, in spite of his three-day blindness, his faith increased as he was greatly used by God's Spirit (Acts 9:8,9).

Just as there cannot be a biological explanation of a kiss, so there can be no psychological analysis of conversion. Nothing can destroy the actual experience of Christ.

With that experience all things are possible. Without it, the church will go limping along like a car with a broken transmission.

To Go Further

Have you been confronted by the living God? Be thankful for that experience.

Are you being confronted now? Are you willing to be?

Can you respond positively? (Acts 9:6)

4th Day Persuasion
Acts 26:19-23

A psychiatrist wrote in the New York Times: "Unless the church gets back to converting the people, we psychiatrists are going to have to do it."

The early church was busy persuading the world about Christ. They who had been converted by the living Christ could not help but share their faith. That's how the fellowship grew so rapidly.

It was not always successful. Paul had been told that he would preach Christ before kings and Gentiles (Acts 9:15). On one such occasion Paul spoke before King Agrippa and the Roman governor, Festus. Neither man was converted on the spot.

It was a great message. The essence is recorded in Acts 26, as Paul shared his personal experience. He told of his vision and the need for obedience to that vision (Acts 26:19). And he spoke eloquently about repentance (Acts 26:20). In spite of persecution he continued to share the gospel (Acts 26:21,22). He was commissioned to go to the Gentile world (Acts 26:23).

You can feel the strength of this man coming through his words. The personal experience on the Damascus road had been the initial thrust to move him into action.

Agrippa and Festus did not respond favorably. Festus thought that Paul was a little disturbed. He insulted him (Acts 26:24). Agrippa was momentarily shaken, but rejected the persuasion of Paul (Acts 26:28).

This did not discourage Paul. He continued with fervor to witness for his faith.

We cannot succeed with everyone. The fact is that we may experience many a failure. If this unduly discourages us, we are done for. We must remember that we are channels and the Holy Spirit will do the work of converting.

We need only be fervent and faithful.

To Go Further

Read Acts 26.

Can you pray about your discouragements?

Are you willing to let the Spirit work through you and in you?

5th Day   Salvation
Acts 9:10-19

Samuel Chadwick, the late principal of Cliff College in Sheffield, Great Britain, tells how the experience of the Holy Spirit came to him while he was not seeking it.

"It came along the line of duty, in a crisis of obedience," he says. He could not explain what had happened, but he became aware of "things unspeakable and full of glory."

There were some results. A deep peace filled his being and a new sense of power. His mind was made alive and he felt that he had a new understanding of spiritual things. He even felt better physically, with a greater sense of vitality and vigor. The experience was real.

"It was as when the Lord Jesus stepped into the boat that with all their rowing had made no progress, and immediately the ship was at the land whither they went."

Salvation is total. It is not only for the soul. It involves the whole of man.

Salvation is of God. He comes to us (Acts

9:3,10). Salvation is a choice (Acts 9:15). Salvation is of the Spirit (Acts 9:17). Salvation opens our physical and spiritual eyes (Acts 9:18).

The reality of the experience becomes ours by faith. Faith does not take our sins away, but faith leads us to Christ who takes our sins away. Faith is not action but taking. Faith is not man's work but our receiving the work of God in our behalf.

"The knowledge He gives is something more than information: it is knowledge that leads to trust, knowledge that brings life, and knowledge that inspires love."*

To Go Further

Do you have a habit of arguing with God? (Acts 9:13,14) What can you do about this?

Are you willing to have your whole person affected by the Holy Spirit? (Acts 9:17) Do you need "salvation" mentally? physically? spiritually?

6th Day   **Declaration**
Romans 1:1-7

Here is a person whose religion is bounded on all sides by negatives. Restrictions. "Thou shalt nots." He picks his way cautiously through life, like a cat walking through a field of broken glass. He avoids

---

*Samuel Chadwick, *The Way to Pentecost;* London: Hodder & Stoughton. Used by Permission.

all the scarlet sins. He is careful not to fall into petty sins. He has it all neatly catalogued—what and what not to do.

So he doesn't commit adultery, at least the outer act itself. He doesn't steal from a store. He attempts to tell the truth and is very blunt; he won't tell a lie. He doesn't play golf on Sundays, and he doesn't go to certain shameful movies. He won't tell dirty stories and keeps from using the Lord's name in vain.

And then he makes one capital mistake. He stops to look at himself, and congratulates himself on his "Christian" life. He has avoided all these pitfalls! He has done quite well in his service to the Lord! He has arrived!

As he congratulates himself he falls flat on his face, because he has been trapped into the worst of all sins—pride, self-righteous pride!

Religion is not this narrow, confining business, although there is certainly a need for self-discipline. But salvation is healing, wholeness, newness in Jesus Christ. It is positive and not negative. It is freeing. It does not imprison a person.

Paul proclaims the gospel of grace and power (Romans 1:4,5). That gospel means literally "good news." It is a call to resurrection and holy living (Romans 1:4). It is a call to sainthood, to enlarged vision, to sonship in God's family.

The joy and enthusiasm of the New Testament can get through to our generation. A prisoner will make others prisoners of his negatives, but a free man will radiate a contagious faith!

To Go Further

What is *your* gospel (Romans 1:4; 2:16)

Are you willing to let God's Spirit change your views? Are you free?

7th Day Communication
Philippians 3:4-11

When the late John F. Kennedy was in the White House, he complained about the use of French on the White House menus.

"When we're having roast beef and mashed potatoes for dinner, why can't we just say so?"

No doubt it sounds more fancy to use French or other languages to puzzle guests for dinner, but why not tell it like it is? Besides, far too often some very fancy titles are given to ordinary dishes!

Do we tend to do the same thing? Do we give some very fancy titles to simple evangelical truth? Can the average man in the street actually understand our terms of justification, sanctification, glorification, or even redemption by the blood of the Lamb?

Only those who are in the know have little trouble with such phrases, but then it becomes a secret language. Was that what the Christian faith was intended to be?

Compare the language Jesus used. How simply He spoke. He expressed eternal truth in words which anyone could understand: home, father, son, vineyard, net, fish, bird, flowers, way, door, sheep and a shepherd.

Why should we complicate what Jesus made so simple?

Paul stripped himself of all that he had gained earlier (Philippians 3:7). He had worked hard to establish a system of thought that would be theologically sound. Now, since his confrontation on the road to Damascus, came the single goal of winning Christ, knowing Him, following Him (Philippians 3:8-10). This he attempted to communicate to everyone (Philippians 3:13,14).

The world will begin to take note again, when what we have made very complicated may be announced in all its essential simplicity as good news.

To Go Further

What words do you use to share the gospel?
Can you study some of Jesus' words?
Can you this day forget and reach? (verse 13)

Make a Decision

After his conversion Paul may have improved his character and given up some bad habits. But, come to think of it, nothing like this is ever mentioned!

What were some of the marks of his conversion?

What are some of the marks of your own? Are you now pointing to certain achievements, or something that is the fruit of the Spirit of God?

Could you make a list of what you expect your experience to do for you—in the future?

CHAPTER 6

When the Fire Spreads

A clergyman from Boston is supposed to have said that he believed in the fatherhood of God, the brotherhood of man, and the neighborhood of Boston.

We may laugh at his provincialism. Are we so much better? Do we believe in the spreading fire of God? Do we take this good news to the ends of the earth?

When the Holy Spirit gets a grip on His church, the fire will spread. It has to. That is one evidence of the presence of the Spirit, and when it is absent, so is the Spirit of God. . . .

Introductory Bible reading for this week: Acts 13–14

"We got down on our knees and put the whole matter in God's hands." C. T. Studd was recounting his call to the mission field. He could not sleep that night. He heard a voice, promising him the heathen for an inheritance. He felt it was the voice of God, and he obeyed the marching orders to "go into all the world."

But many people said that he was making a huge mistake. Why should an educated, intelligent, accomplished national champion like C. T. bury himself in the interior of some far-off country? He would have great influence with the young men of England. They all knew him by name.

Perhaps, said Studd, the devil used the same argument with Moses. "Why don't you stay in the palace? You will have more influence among your peers." But Moses followed the call of God and brought his people to freedom.

Before he went to the mission field, C. T. Studd did speak of his decision at some universities and a revival broke forth among the students of every university in England! One man was obedient, and the result was an awakening "the like of which has never been seen before or since."

It is a lonely trek when you follow God's appointment. Not much glamor. Not many honors. Not much applause. But who can measure the spiritual influence that will be exerted because you are faithful?

God's guidance is mysterious, but it has meaning

and direction. We may not know the reason why, but we can obey. When we pray for His direction, there will be an answer (Acts 1:24). The answer will be clear and obvious (Acts 1:26).

That's how the fire will spread.

To Go Further

Have you honestly prayed for guidance?
Do you believe you can receive it?
Are you willing to act on it when you do?
Meditate on Philippians 3:15,16.

2nd Day   **How the Holy Spirit Leads**
Acts 13:1-5

"The mission of the church is missions."

"This generation can only reach this generation."

"The church that gives is the church that lives."

These are some of the mottoes of the famous People's Church in Toronto, Canada, where the pastor Oswald J. Smith often said that he had no objection to people hearing the gospel a thousand times, but they had no excuse for not proclaiming it to people who had never heard it once.

The early Christians were a contagious lot because the Holy Spirit had His way with them. God is the source of missions (Acts 13:2). It was not Paul's idea or Barnabas'. It did not come from man, but from the Spirit of God. Just as the gospel was the revelation of God to man, so the missionary movement began as a vertical force.

The men whom God chose for this work were the leaders of the church. It may have seemed to those Christians at Antioch that Paul and Barnabas were indispensable to the cause of Christ *there*. Why should they have to give up the most able teachers of the Word? Could they not have had a greater influence if they remained at Antioch? Why not send some others?

But they had already been called (verse 2). And their call was not to remain forever at Antioch. They had been commissioned to consider the whole world as their parish.

God's neighborhood is not Boston.

There was fasting and prayer in that church (Acts 13:3). Would you consider this the secret of the missionaries' success?

The more we study in the Acts of the Apostles, the more we will be led into that spiritual awakening which the world needs. Nor can anything be accomplished apart from our faith and willingness to be led of the Spirit.

To Go Further

Study Job 22:21,22 for guidance.
Are you open to the leading of the Spirit?
What does He want you to respond to today?

There can be no fire without a spark. There can be no blaze without an initial fire.

There will be no witness on the part of the church without the Holy Spirit. There will be no enthusiasm or contagion without the power of God.

They had first to receive the power (Acts 1:8). The power is the Holy Spirit Himself. The Spirit would come upon them, and *then* they would proclaim Christ throughout the world.

So the item on the agenda for the church is to receive the power of God, to believe the promise of Christ, to pray for its fulfillment and to be open to the influx of the Spirit. The apostles believed, they prayed, they waited, and the power came. There is no other way.

In 1950 two men climbed the mountain called Annapurna, 26,000 feet high. It was the highest mountain to be scaled at that point in history. When Maurice Herzog and his companion finally reached the top after a tremendous effort, they felt emotions which they attempted to describe.

"Our hearts overflowed with an unspeakable happiness, and we found ourselves saying, 'If only the others could know. If only everyone could know.'"

Haven't you had a desire to share something exhilarating, something magnificent, something wonderful in your experience? Or even have a desire to tell about some remedy for a cold, or a recipe that has been a favorite of yours?

73

If your conversion has been real, if your experience of Christ has been genuine, if you have received the Holy Spirit, *the experience itself* will motivate you to tell others. "If only everyone could know." That's how a Christian feels about it.

To Go Further

What is the connection between the ascension of Jesus and the descent of the Spirit? (Acts 1:9-11; 2:4)
What may be blocking God's power in your life?
What are you willing to do about it?

4th Day   How God Opens Our Eyes
Acts 16:6-10

"Does it bother you to think that there may be people around who dislike you?" Charlie Brown asked Lucy.

"Dislike *me?*" said Lucy with that incredulous look on her face. "How could anyone possibly dislike me? There's nothing to dislike!"

A finger came up to her face, and she continued her thoughts: "Jealous, maybe . . . yes, I could understand that. . . . I can see how someone could be jealous of me . . . but dislike? No, that's just not possible."

She turned to Charlie: "So, getting back to your original question . . ."

"Forget it," said Charlie Brown.

Obviously Charlie was trying to tell Lucy something. But she wouldn't listen. Her mind was closed. She did not afford herself the luxury of exploring the possibility that all was not as it ought to have been.

When God opens our eyes, we cannot hide any longer. We may not like what we see, but we can only act—unless we prefer to remain spiritually blind.

It was plain that God had other plans for Paul (Acts 16:6,7). Then at Troas there was a direct revelation (Acts 16:9). Now he had a choice: to do what he wanted to do, or to follow the revelation of the Spirit of God. Again, as at his conversion, he was obedient to the heavenly vision (Acts 16:10). So the gospel came to Europe for the first time.

A neurotic person is one who is overly preoccupied with himself. A neurotic church is more concerned with maintenance than with mission. It is always probing inward without reaching outward.

The fire will spread, when, having opened our eyes, we are obedient to the heavenly vision.

To Go Further

Read Galatians 5:17-26.
What does that lead you to pray for? to do?
Are you able to come to Christ in honesty?
What specifically are you to do today?

Take a look at Asia. That great continent has approximately 60,864,000 Christians, of which only 10,908,000 are Protestants.

But there are in Asia 1,867,000,000 people. (Figures are based on the 1969 Almanac.) And that means that only 3.2% are Christians, less than 1% Protestants.

India has the most Christians, almost 9,000,000. But India also has a population of 511,115,000. Therefore the percentage is only 1.7%. The highest percentage of Christians is in New Guinea, where twenty percent of the population has responded to the good news. The Philippines are next with ten percent.

After all these years of missionary endeavor it is an eye-opener to discover that less than one percent of the population of Asia has been reached with the good news.

Add to this fact the report of *Christianity Today* that there is only one missionary for every 118,000 people, and then ask yourself what God's Spirit may be saying to His church in our time.

Or consider the fact that one denomination asked for four hundred missionaries, received ninety applications on which they could act favorably, but then could only send seventy. Why? Not enough funds!

The time has come to receive the Spirit (John 20:22). The Lord will send us into His world (John 20:21). As the Father sent the Son for our salvation, so we are to respond to His call into *all* the world.

Should we be building walls or bridges?

To Go Further

What is the meaning of John 20:22?
What is the meaning of John 20:23?
Meditate on the words of John 20:21.
Receiving is a matter of taking. Let God's Spirit remove your fears, and take charge of your life.

6th Day How to Be Faithful
Acts 28:23-28

One of our troubles is that we don't debate with the evil, the sordid, the wrong. But we do debate with the good. Should we do this or not? Is it really necessary?

All such debate, as Peter did when the vision was given to him (Acts 10:14), hinders the operation of the Spirit of God in our lives.

Paul continued in faithfulness. He did not debate the issues with God. Some believed and others rejected the gospel (Acts 28:24). That did not stop him. He was not called upon to become a success. He was called upon to be God's man.

He knew the Scriptures (Acts 28:25-28). The plain words of Isaiah did not dry up his enthusiasm for Christ. He turned instead to the Gentile world with the message (Acts 28:28).

Neither could persecution and imprisonment stop him. When the Holy Spirit had hold of him, that was enough. He continued to preach and to teach (Acts 28:31). On that joyous note the book of the Acts closes. It tells the same story from beginning to end. The Spirit came, and He was directing the activity of the Christians.

There are some very human causes of failure among missionaries. Number one on the list, so say the mission boards, is an unwillingness to work harmoniously with others. Number two is not far behind: a feeling of superiority to the nationals. The third largest cause for failure is the inability to submit to mission disciplines.

Friction between husband and wife, an unsatisfactory devotional life, a lack of personal cleanliness and slovenly work habits also contributed to many failures, not to mention problems of sex.

That's another way of saying that some people may be missionaries (or ministers or teachers) who are not willing to give the Holy Spirit priority in their lives.

To Go Further

Are you able to withstand the disappointments?

Are you being led by the Holy Spirit?

What specific, very human step should you take today?

Ninety-seven percent of India remains non-Christian. Eighty percent is probably out of touch with the gospel. If that is the situation, how could we possibly say that the task is complete and the missionaries ought to be withdrawn?

What the Indian Christians really want is not missionaries who will bring technical expertise. They want men and women of missionary passion who are leaders who will go and bring Christ to the people. The Indian church wants to be trained so that they can join in the task of making Christ known to their people.

"This then is the picture of the missionary's task today," said Lesslie Newbigin in an address to the American church. "He is the indispensable personal expression of the duty and privilege of the whole church in every land to take the whole gospel of salvation to the whole world, and to prepare the world for the coming of its sovereign Lord."

It all began in that vital fellowship which was infused with the Spirit of God. He directed their missionary endeavors. God worked through a man like Peter who was not ashamed to battle his prejudices and who accepted the challenge to witness to a member of another race (Acts 10:34,35). The message was the same (Acts 10:36). Peter called on his hearers to face Christ either as Judge or Saviour (Acts 10:42,43).

There is no reason why the church should have allowed itself to be derailed. Nor is there a reason why we should remain as ineffective and insipid as we have recently become. God still wants to use His church. He wants to work through His people. His power is available. The story need never end. It can and ought to be continued!

"Behold, I have set before thee an open door" (Revelation 3:8).

To Go Further

Don't dream about being a missionary some day. Report for service today!

Since you won't be judged for where you have not been, how is it where you *have* been?

Are you willing to be used by God's Spirit?

Make a Decision

Some people become missionaries because they have a martyr complex. They are trying to make it up to God.

Some go for humanitarian reasons and, like many in the Peace Corps, don't last long.

Others have a sense of responsibility to a pushy parent or even a pastor's or someone else's influence.

For what reason are you a Christian? Do you feel any *pressure* to witness? Who is exerting this pressure on you?

Examine honestly your motivations. If you have sinned confess it to God. Be open to the Spirit of God.

CHAPTER 7

What Is Your Gospel?

"If only I had seen Jesus! If only I had been there with Him, as those apostles were. If only I had one single day with Him, all my problems would be solved, all my confusion would be gone."

Has that thought ever crossed your mind? It is only natural. Yet, what does this do to the whole biblical emphasis on the Holy Spirit? Is not the teaching of Jesus that the Spirit is now let loose in the world? "Ye shall receive power" (Acts 1:8)!

When you receive the Holy Spirit in your life you have all the power you need to do the Lord's work as He directs you.

Introductory Bible reading for this week: Acts 15:1-35; Galatians 2

1st Day **A Matter of Experience**
Galatians 1:10-24

He was no atheist. He was a devout believer in
God. He was no casual Jew. He spent his time in
zealously protecting his religion, even to the point
of exterminating that Christian heresy. He could
not tolerate any breach of the traditions (Galatians
1:13,14).

But the overwhelming revelation that came to
him on that road to Damascus turned his life
around. God took the initiative and called him
(Galatians 1:15). It was all the grace of God
through faith in Jesus Christ.

Not only did God reveal Jesus *to* Paul, the revelation was *in* him. A matter of personal experience,
a subjective realization not merely an objective
fact.

How personal was the continued revelation
(Galatians 1:16-18). Paul had to do an about-face
in his theology. His whole system of thought had to
be changed from salvation by law to justification
by faith, from righteousness achieved by good
works to accepting righteousness by the grace of
God alone.

But when he really met Christ, the result was obvious to the Christian community (Galatians
1:23,24).

We need always to begin here, although it never
ends here. The beginning is in the personal experience of the living Christ. The end is in allowing the
Spirit to channel His power through you: "That I

might preach him among the heathen" (Galatians 1:16).

Do you have this certainty? Could you write a similar chapter to Galatians 1 in your own words? Is it the very foundation of your personal faith that Christ and you have met? Are these mere words or spiritual realities?

To Go Further

Is your faith personal? How can it be?

Can you say it in the positive way Paul writes Galatians 1:16? And can you add verse 20?

Write out your own personal experience, bringing it up-to-date.

2nd Day   **By the Grace of God**
Romans 11:1-6

The word "salvation" is like the cross that purchased it. It reaches up to heaven and opens our communication with God. It goes down into hell and delivers us from the penalty of sin. It embraces the whole world, "for God so loved the world, that he gave" (John 3:16).

For the past there is forgiveness. In the present there is power and in the future, life forever.

You do not earn salvation, it is given. You do not buy it, it is not for sale. You cannot achieve it, it must be received. It is the free gift of God. This is the good news (Romans 11:6).

It is often assumed that only Gentiles have responded to this message. That is not true (Romans 11:1). The first Christians were Jews. Even when Paul experienced the rejection in synagogue after synagogue and went to the Gentile world, there were continually Jews who were responding to the gospel. So it has been through history (Romans 11:2). There is always a remnant (Romans 11:5).

The gospel is for all men. Paul makes a special point of this in his desire to reach the world (Romans 1:16). Since Jesus died for the world, it is the world that is to hear the message of salvation.

How well you may think you know the old, old story of Jesus and His love, there is no end in discovering how much you still have to think about. You will never come to the end of all you can find in the grace of God. By that free, forgiving love you can live. Without it you can never be free.

It is no wonder, then, that when the pure gospel is proclaimed, the Holy Spirit will do His work in the world. And when men really hear that good news, they find it difficult to reject God's free offer of love.

What else is there, after all?

To Go Further

Meditate on Romans 6:6.
Let God's grace fill your soul today.
Experience its cleansing power.
Gain a new perspective on life.

The questions pile up.

If you are a Christian, why do you veer from your faith? If you believe in the cross of Christ, why should you look in another direction? If you have heard the truth, why do you so easily get removed from the truth (Galatians 3:1)? Hasn't it been enough for you that the cross was placarded before you as the only way of salvation?

How did you receive the Holy Spirit? Was it a matter of achievement? Did you work for it? Was the Holy Spirit given to you because you had kept every detail of the law? Or did the Spirit come to you because you believed (Galatians 3:2)?

Paul takes it for granted that the Spirit has been given to the Galatians, and that He came because of their initial faith. We sing "Pass me not, O gentle Saviour"; as if He would. . . . There is a certainty born of faith.

And still more questions.

How are you to grow? What is the secret of living the Christian life? Is it possible to accomplish by self-effort? Can the flesh complete what the Spirit began? If faith were needed to receive the grace of God, then why should faith no longer be a necessity in the Christian life (Galatians 3:3)?

Besides, did not your Christian testimony lead to suffering? Were you readily received by your former friends when you shared with them your newfound faith? Did they appreciate some of the changes in your life? Were all these painful experiences for nothing (Galatians 3:4)?

Therefore consider whether the Spirit of God who is working in and through your fellowship does this because of the works of the law, or because of sheer faith (Galatians 3:5).

When you probe into the heart of the gospel of faith in Christ, you discover the dynamic and direction for Christian living and action.

To Go Further

Study the case of Abraham. (Galatians 3:6-9)

What does it mean to live by faith and not in the flesh?

Is the Holy Spirit showing you anything to do today?

4th Day In the Power of the Spirit
Romans 8:1-8

There is that old story about Sisyphus. He kept on pushing a rock up a hill, but he never did get it over the top. Every time he neared the summit he kept on saying to himself: "This time I will do it. Steady now. I'm almost there. This time. . . ."

But the effort was too great. The task was impossible, and that massive rock would come rolling down again. He had to start anew.

Are we intended to be morally impotent like Sisyphus? Can we gain the victory? Can we overcome our temptations? Are we ever to be free from our besetting sins?

Unless that answer is positive, we will be inwardly defeated as we attempt to share Christ. Such inner defeat can only result in a detriment to our witness. So, if the church is to awaken to its task in the world, it will be accomplished when we win our moral victories in Christ.

But this is the work of God's Spirit. We are not in the flesh, but are to live in that Spirit (Romans 8:4). Since we are no longer under condemnation, we should begin to breathe in this freedom (Romans 8:1,2). Sin is condemned and so is the flesh (Romans 8:3). The carnal mind leads to death and the spiritual mind to peace (Romans 8:6).

This is Scripture. It is the inspired and revealed Word of God. Can we believe it?

This is the work of the Holy Spirit. He has been given to us, the moment we believed. He can make us spiritually minded. He will bring us to life and peace. Do we believe this?

There will be ultimate and final victory for us—one day. Old things will pass away, and all things will be made new (Revelation 21:5). Can we not begin to taste this victory by faith *now*? Do we believe it?

To Go Further

Bring your particular temptation to Christ. Don't be afraid. Lay it out before Him. Don't shy away from it. He knows it anyway.

Now can you apply, believe and commit yourself to Romans 8:5,6, prayerfully?

Titus 3:1-8

Christianity is more than a philosophy of life, although it will give you that. This Christian faith is ultimately the only thing that will make sense out of the universe. But you need more than a philosophy of life to hold you steady when the storms begin to blow and temptation strikes.

Christianity is more than a moral code, although it will give you the finest ethic in the world. But you cannot be set on fire by something that is as cold and distant as moral maxims.

Nor is Christianity a social creed, although it will give you that too. The Christian faith has been responsible for more social reforms than we can enumerate. But no amount of social involvement can change a life and work the miracle of new birth.

The essence of Christianity is a personal response to the good news of Christ. It is a matter of experience and faith.

"That is religion—not a vague abstraction, but a wonderful affection; not a tiresome argument, but a tremendous friendship; not an intricate and uninspired philosophy, but an inspired and thrilling love; not a drudging at the grindstone of a dingy routine morality, but 'Christ in you the hope of glory.'"*

"Regeneration . . . renewing" (Titus 3:5)! Great words. Our Saviour has appeared and we are saved

---

*James S. Stewart, *The Gates of New Life*, Edinburgh: T. & T. Clark. Page 126.

through His mercy (Titus 3:4,5). There is a washing away of our sins, and as a result, a new relationship, a new dynamic, a new beginning. Inner renewal through faith in God's grace.

That is Christianity. Anything else is a pale reflection of the real thing.

To Go Further

Why this emphasis on good works? (Titus 3:1,8)

In what way do you need renewing?

What is the relationship between grace and works?

Can you pray in specifics today?

6th Day   **Sober and Zealous**
Titus 2:11-15

The drone bee (male) does nothing for the hive. He has all the leisure time in the world. He enters the hive and leaves it at will, without any responsibility whatsoever. He has the freedom to visit any hive he wishes, and he can supervise the activities. The bees do all the work. The drone does nothing.

But when summer ends, his time of eating and loafing is up, too. They take him to the front of the beehive and clip his wings. Not long thereafter, he dies.

There are some Christians who rest easy on the grace of God. They live without any responsibility.

They go in and out of the church, supervising some particular committee, but they only take.

It's too bad that we don't treat them as bees treat the drone, and clip their wings if they will not join in the building of the kingdom of God.

The grace of God has appeared (Titus 2:11). But why? For what reason? That we may loaf our way into heaven, since we can't work for it anyway? Is that the implication of the grace of God?

The very opposite is the case. The grace of God has appeared and teaches us to deny ungodliness and worldly lusts (Titus 2:12). That demands effort. And it has appeared to lead us into positive, zealous good works (Titus 2:12).

Good works are never done in behalf of our salvation. They are the result of God's mercy toward us. We are redeemed in order to be zealous of good works (Titus 2:14).

If we believe in the blessed hope of the return of Christ, should this not lead us to prepare for Him (Titus 2:13)?

What is *your* gospel?

To Go Further

Pray and meditate carefully through this passage in Titus 2:11-15. Consider every aspect.

What is God's Spirit leading you to confess?

What does He want from you in action, today?

"The only faith which makes a Christian is that which casts itself on God for life or death," said Martin Luther.

It is so easy to be sentimental about the gospel. To sing hymns without ever considering the words we sing. To repeat familiar phrases without realizing their implications in life. To go through the motions without touching the heart of things.

We can offer beautiful prayers for the offering and toss a few cents in the plate. We can promise to serve Christ in any way, and neglect to carry out some responsibility that is given to us. We can spout off about our faith and cling to some inner resentment, some hostility, refusing to forgive someone for an injury to us.

We can talk about love and be utterly loveless. We can emote about peace and be continually anxious. We can tell others about victory and remain inwardly defeated.

All this is not the mark of a Christian. It is not in the language we use, no matter how glowing or "true to the Word." It is only in the full surrender, in the commitment to the Christ who died on the cross for us. Christianity is life in the Spirit. Christianity is faith from the heart.

This is the word of faith (Romans 10:8). This is a matter of the heart (Romans 10:9). You make not only the orthodox confession, but you make it from the heart (Romans 10:10).

Let us not be satisfied with a Christianity that is

so easy, that it leads into laziness and abuse of the grace of God. Let it be the faith which "casts itself on God for life or death." So shall the church be renewed and used of the Spirit.

To Go Further

Compare the two types of righteousness. (Romans 10:3-6)

What is the real meaning of faith?

As they used to ask in days gone by: "Is your heart right with God?"

Make a Decision

When Jesus was on trial before Pilate, He asked the Roman governor whether his information was his own or hearsay. "Is that your own idea, or have others suggested it to you" (John 18:34, N.E.B.)?*

That is your question too. What you affirm about Christ—is it yours or are you merely repeating what others have said? Is it your own experience or a hand-me-down? Is it personal discovery or repetition of orthodox creeds?

Never be satisfied to replace firsthand experience with secondhand tradition.

*From *The New English Bible,* © The Delegates of the Oxford University Press and the Syndics of the Cambridge University Press, 1961.

CHAPTER 8

Pagan World, Here We Come

A successful doctor practicing in New York City had achieved everything he ever dreamed of. But he said: "All my success seems like an overripe apple and rotting in my hands."

A leading world diplomat asked Billy Graham in privacy whether he knew how to find inner peace.

That pagan world around us is a needy world. It is torn by strife and tension, by dissatisfaction and disappointment, by restlessness and greed. And always that inner, gnawing emptiness.

Our Lord calls us into that world. Pagan world, here we come!

Introductory Bible reading for this week: Acts 17:16-33; 19:23-41; I Peter 3:13-17

"Science is my shepherd, I shall not want.
He maketh me to lie down on foam rubber cush-
    ions.
He leadeth me beside the superhighways,
He leadeth me in the paths of psychoanalysis for
    peace of mind's sake.
Yea, though I walk through the valley of the shad-
    ow I will fear no evil for science is my savior.
He prepareth a table before me in the presence of
    the world's billions of hungry people.
My beer glass foameth over.
He anointeth my head with home permanents.
Surely pleasure and prosperity shall follow me all
    the days of my life,
And I shall dwell in Shangri-La forever."

—Anonymous

Far-fetched? Perhaps. But this pagan world
serves many masters while it remains ignorant of
the true Lord. It follows many roads while it is
blind to the Way. It bows before many idols and
rebels against the God of the universe.

But this is a visited world. The Light has come.
The glory of God has been revealed in Jesus Christ
(Isaiah 60:1). He, who is the Light of the world,
has not been put out by the darkness (Isaiah 60:2;
John 1:5). And the end is not yet in sight, for kings
shall come to that Light and the nations will enter
into glory (Isaiah 60:3,5-7; Revelation 21:26).

So, no matter how loud the noise against us, no

94

matter how rebellious man pursues his false gods, pagan world—here we come! We come with the good news. We come in the power of the Spirit. We come because we cannot do otherwise. "All power is given unto me in heaven and in earth. Go ye therefore" (Matthew 28:18,19).

To Go Further

Do you have this vision which Isaiah presents?
Read through John 1:1-14.
If the world in its rebellion overwhelms you, can you gain inner strength from the Spirit—today?

2nd Day   In the Foolishness of Preaching
I Corinthians 1:18-25

A famous acrobat from Europe walked across Niagara Falls on a wire. Then he walked back as the crowd applauded generously. Not only had he accomplished the feat in the face of danger, but he had held steady against the winds.

He turned to the people: "Do you believe in me?"

They replied in one voice: "Yes."

"Then if you believe in me," said the acrobat, "who will come and ride on my shoulders as I cross again?"

There was no reply.

"Don't you believe in me?"

Finally a tall farm boy stepped forward and rode on his shoulders across the Niagara.

In the foolishness of preaching we ask for faith in Jesus Christ—the Christ who has demonstrated for us the power of salvation. The Christ who has removed from us the penalty of sin. The Christ who has walked across the abyss of death and come back from the other side in resurrection glory.

The preaching of this cross may seem like foolishness (I Corinthians 1:18). But to us who put our trust in the atonement, it is power. The preaching of the cross is not a philosophy which man can approve (I Corinthians 1:19). It is the wisdom of redemption and the revelation of the grace of God (I Corinthians 1:21).

We can only announce it. We can only tell the story. We can only proclaim it. That is the meaning of the word *preaching*, which appears so often in these verses.

That proclamation can lead to our salvation. It can and will rescue us from meaningless despair, from guilt and sin, from death and hell. It may not appear wise, but God's wisdom far exceeds the philosophies of men (I Corinthians 1:25).

We confront the pagan world with no other message than that of the crucified and risen Lord.

To Go Further

How is this gospel a stumbling block to people? (verse 23)

96

Why is it foolishness? (verse 23)
Are you persuaded of its power? (verse 18)

3rd Day **In the Power of God**
I Corinthians 2:6-16

"Thoughts hardly to be packed
Into a narrow act,
Fancies that broke through language and
    escaped..."

So wrote Robert Browning as he attempted to
tell us that there are some things we cannot fully
capture in words. They have to break *through* our
language and escape.

Bernard of Clairvaux said the same in that familiar hymn:

"Nor tongue nor pen can show;
The love of Jesus, what it is,
None but His loved ones know."

What is a rainbow? Can you describe it in a
complicated equation about the laws of light? Can
you capture it in words? Or is the magic, the
wonder, the poetry of a rainbow beyond human expression?

Paul is often caught up in that same problem. He
attempted to tell the love of Jesus, what it is, but
he had to stop short (I Corinthians 2:9). The Holy
Spirit must reveal the eternal things of God, for
man cannot do it (I Corinthians 2:10,11). So the
message we preach is not the result of human wisdom but the teaching of the Spirit of God (I Corinthians 2:13).

97

No wonder this is difficult to comprehend (I Corinthians 2:14). It is not of man but of God. It is not human wisdom but divine revelation. It is not man's discovery but truth from above.

We come to that pagan world in the power of God with the wisdom of God, led by the Spirit of God. That is a mystery (I Corinthians 2:7). The mystery of Christ led to the crucifixion (I Corinthians 2:8). Since, therefore, these are the things of the Spirit, they can only be discerned spiritually.

But, like a rainbow, or a poem, we can experience what we may not be able to express in words.

To Go Further

Are you really open to the Spirit of God?
Are these simply words to you, or actualities?
Meditate particularly on verses 10-14.

4th Day   **In the Name of Jesus**
Acts 16:16-24

In the early days of the evangelization of China there was a severe famine. The Christian leaders went into the fields to help cut rice and distribute it to the starving. The first day, one in every seven persons asked them about Jesus. The leaders excused themselves and said they had no time to talk to them, since they were busy distributing rice.

But the next day they were better organized.

They put up a tent and marked it "evangelist." Then when the requests came, the Christians merely pointed to the tent and urged the people to talk to the evangelist. Invariably they received one answer: "We don't want to hear from the man in the tent, but from you . . . because you care. . . ."

We have taken the street clothes off Jesus and put ecclesiastical robes on Him. We have removed Him from His ministry among the common people and shut Him up in our churches. We keep on pointing people to the doors of the church, rather than to Jesus Himself.

Jesus was *there* among the people in His earthly ministry. Some came to Him while He was in the synagogue, to be sure. But the majority of His contacts were on the road.

If the church is to come alive as it did in the first century it must go in the name of Jesus to the people—on the streets, in the homes, at the offices, in the schools, to the hospitals, yes, even to the prisons. The early Christians often found themselves there. And it wasn't easy for them.

We live in a world which has used up every option imaginable. The only option left is Jesus Christ, the Way, the Truth and the Life (John 14:6). Let us go in the name of Jesus, and where they are, tell the good news.

To Go Further

Is there someone specific who comes to your mind today?

Will you write a letter or make a call in the name of Jesus and for His sake?

Pray about it.

In the novel *Vanessa* by Hugh Walpole, a young man is talking to his mother about Vanessa.

"Vanessa is so good and so fine. She believes in God, you know, Mother," he says.

"And don't you?" she asks him incredulously.

"You know that I don't," he replies. "Not as she does. Not as she does. I may be wrong. I dare say I am. But I *must* be honest. I don't see things that way. I'm ignorant. I don't know any more than the next fellow and I want the next fellow to believe as he sees, but I must be allowed to see for myself."

He stops for a moment, and then continues as he gets to his main problem:

"I can't *see* God anywhere. The things that people believe are fine for them but nonsense to me. To me as I am now. I've got all my life in front of me and everything to learn. God may be proved to me yet. I hope He will be."

"Proved!" his mother replies. "God can't be proved, Benjie. He must be felt."

"Yes, I suppose so. That may come to me one day. Meanwhile—a heathen and a vagabond can't marry Vanessa."

You can't *see* God anywhere? That for many pa-

100

gans is the problem, and they hope for some demonstration. If they do not get it, they are not likely to take up Christianity.

We cannot confront the pagan world with proofs and evidences. It is a question of faith. It is a matter of experience. It comes down to the willingness of the individual to turn to Jesus Christ. It is a matter of choice.

Once a person makes that choice, some evidence and proof *may* follow. But faith is not faith if it is based on sight.

That has been the issue in Paul's letter to the Romans (10:3-10,16,17). It is the reason for the fall of Israel as a nation (Romans 11:11,12). And those Gentiles who respond are only "in" because of their faith (Romans 11:20).

To Go Further

Pray about that person who comes to your mind.

Ask for new direction to witness to him or her.

Realize anew that you stand only by grace. (Romans 11:6,18-20)

6th Day **With Assurance of Victory**
Revelation 22:1-5

The pagan world has its limitations. It will not always endure. There will be a new city, with a pure river, and the streets will be filled with the redeemed (Revelation 22:1,2). The nations will be healed of their sickness and sin (verse 2). There will be no darkness and the former curse will be gone (verses 3-5).

This is the goal. This is where we are headed. All things will become new.

If we can gain this perspective from Scripture, we will be encouraged to go into this pagan world by the power of God. Our message will bring hope and certainty, for we are assured of the ultimate victory.

Thomas Chalmers had been content for years to preach a cold, dry, formal religion with utmost precision. But then in his church manse, an experience of the living Christ shook this great Christian preacher and he said: "Mathematician that I was, I had forgotten two magnitudes—the shortness of time and the vastness of eternity."

Pagan world, here we come! We can do no other. Eternity is hard upon us. We are here but for a moment. And we cannot avoid that day of reckoning. This is the hour for the gospel of Christ, and we must make the most of it.

C. E. Montague has a few words written somewhere which should cause us to think about all of Scripture: "All the best part of experience consists in discovering that perfectly trite pieces of observation are shiningly and exhilaratingly true."

Of course, nothing in Scripture is ever trite. But our *observation* of it is wanting, and when like Thomas Chalmers we see the shortness of time and the vastness of eternity with new eyes, we will indeed be awakened from our sleepy churchianity.

To Go Further

You can't duplicate the experience of another, but you can meditate on time and eternity. . . .

Pray that the Spirit will make simple things "shiningly and exhilaratingly true" for you!

7th Day   To Serve the Living God
I Thessalonians 1:2-10

Someone has said that there are lily Christians—they toil not, neither do they spin.

How different was Paul's description of the Christians in Thessalonica, a town in the north of Greece. He spoke of their work of faith, their labor of love and their patience of hope (I Thessalonians 1:3).

Because they were aware of their election and choice by God, and because they had received the power of the Holy Spirit, they actively lived out their faith in that pagan world around them (verses 4,5). That involved suffering (verse 6). But they were joyous in persecution, because the Holy Spirit was at work within them. So much so, that many Christians had heard of their vibrant faith (verse 7).

"From you sounded out the word of the Lord" (verse 8). That was the dynamic in the early church. They were not ingrown. They were concerned, and out of that concern they shared the good news.

The deliverance from false gods had been such a reality (verse 9) that they could not help but serve the living God. From dumb idols to the God who has spoken in His Son. From false idols to the true God.

As servants belong to their master, so these Christians belonged to their Lord. They allowed Him full sway in their lives. They were willing and obedient. Not perfect by any means. Just willing to allow God's Spirit to use them in His service.

A campus sign recently carried the words: Jesus —YES. Christianity—NO. Why? What has happened within the Christian church that such is the reaction of the pagan world to us?

Let it be a hopeful sign that it is still Jesus—*yes*. Let us confront the pagan world in the name of Jesus and in the power of God!

To Go Further

Are you willing to serve without rewards?

Are you willing to serve if it leads to persecution for you?

Is I Thessalonians 1:7,8 true for you?

Make a Decision

What can you do about this pagan world?

You can begin to pray. Prayer will open the door that was locked for you, and you may be amazed at the ease of approach to someone for whom you pray regularly.

You can be a friend. It is not outside our friendships but in them that Christ can be found. Not as often with strangers as with those who trust us.

You can be loving, expressing God's love in the power of the Spirit (Galatians 5:22). *Serve.* Give a cup of cold water in Jesus' name. Visit the afflicted. Give yourself to the needy.

What will be your decision?

CHAPTER 9

The Newness of the New

A Christianity that has become fat and compla-
cent needs, among other things, a reducing diet. It
needs to take the vitamins of the Spirit and feed on
the Bread of life. It needs to get back to basic
(foods) and stay away from those fat-producing
calories.

Christianity with a middle-aged spread is not appealing. Can we recapture the vitality of youth, the
enthusiasm and dedication of that youthful church
that lived and moved through the first century with
the dynamic of the Spirit?

This is our only hope.

Introductory Bible reading for this week: Hebrews 8:1–10:18

"The Rebel" is a book by Albert Camus. In this book which probes deeply into human nature and the problems of man in God's world, the French author states that man has only two choices: the sacred, or rebellion to it.

Nothing in between. Either man is an unbeliever, or he believes. Either man is anti-God or he is God's man. Either he is for, or else he is against. There is no middle ground.

"Only two possible worlds can exist for the human mind . . . the sacred or the world of rebellion."

What is your world? Do you believe or do you mock? Do you accept or do you reject? Do you worship or do you resist? Most people pass through a rebellious stage in life, but that's no way to end up. It is generally considered juvenile behavior, and hardly the mark of an adult.

There is always a division presented in the Bible (Deuteronomy 7:9,10). It is either/or. No in between. But *because* God loved, *because* He has made a covenant, *because* He is faithful, we can be assured of His presence and love (Deuteronomy 7:8).

There are responsibilities for us who belong to Him, who are His people. These responsibilities are represented in action verbs: "hear" . . . "learn" . . . "keep" . . . "do" (Deuteronomy 5:1). And again, "keep" . . . "do" (Deuteronomy 7:11). All this is the result of His redemption (Deuteronomy 7:8). The redemption of the covenant-keeping God becomes the motivation for Christian action.

Since our challenge is to bring about change in people, and therefore in situations, it can only come about through dedicated, believing, redeemed Christians. Christians who are not afraid to enter into the patient task in the Spirit, of making men whole.

To Go Further

Realize anew the love of God. (Deuteronomy 7:7,8)

Analyze your own attitudes: rebel or obedient?

Ask to be made right in your motives.

2nd Day   **The Compassionate God**
Hosea 11:1-9

A gambler says that unless there's a little money on a game, he won't even play. He wouldn't sit down to a game of cards or roll the dice, unless there's something to be gained. Money, that is. And the more the better.

Apparently it's like that. The higher the stakes, the more "fun" in the game. The greater the danger too!

So is life. Everything is at stake. You gamble your life on God or no God. On eternity or extinction. Heaven or hell. The stakes are way up there—

your whole life! And there's no turning back. "What shall it profit a man, if he shall gain the whole world, and lose his own soul" (Mark 8:36)?

There is one reason why you can safely gamble your life on God. The love of God! His compassion. His mercy. His grace.

Hosea was a man who experienced that love and became an expression of it as well. His wife had been unfaithful to him. He took her back. Not once, but several times.

Hosea expressed the love of God for Israel (Hosea 11:1). That love was deep and real (verse 4). And in spite of the people's continual backsliding, God would not give them up (verses 7,8).

How do you feel about a God like that? How do you respond to a covenant-keeping God who is compassionate and merciful above and beyond anything you deserve? How do you respond to a God who sends His only Son into the world, rejected and meek, to die on a cross? Doesn't that move you at all?

Life is a gamble. But if that is the way Christians throughout the years have experienced the living God—why not stick with the winners?

To Go Further

Read the entire book of Hosea.
Meditate on the compassion of God.
Let His love lead you into fresh expressions of faith.

The young man told the pastor what was on his mind. He had wronged a girl who had been a servant in their home. He was wealthy and got off scot-free. She was left with her shame and sent away.

He had told his story to another counselor, who had said: "Brother, all you have to do about it is confess to God, and Calvary will cover it."

The pastor to whom he was telling his story said: "No more damnable advice was ever forged on the anvils of hell than that!" Calvary will never cover what we have to uncover.

The young man confessed that he was still troubled about the affair and, despite the advice of the first counselor, could not quiet his own conscience. The pastor then told him to write to the girl, to her parents and to his own parents. To confess, to tell the whole story, and to assume his part in helping the situation. When those three letters were mailed, that fellow experienced a sense of relief.

God is our Saviour, but there can be no shortcut to salvation. We cannot buy that salvation by anything we accomplish (Isaiah 55:1). But we must forsake our wicked way and our unrighteous thoughts (Isaiah 55:7). There can be no mercy unless we are willing to do that (Isaiah 55:8).

The Lord is not able to use a sick church which refuses to take the road of honest repentance. Secret sins must be secretly confessed. Public sins must be publicly confessed. And when another person or persons are involved, restitution must be made.

People will be saved only when Christians will become what they ought to be—men and women of integrity and honesty and truthfulness, men and women of the *Holy* Spirit of God.

To Go Further

What have you covered that needs to be uncovered? Can you pray for power to do it?

Trust God for His promise. (Isaiah 55:7)

Believe that His Word will bring about joy, if you follow it. (Isaiah 55:11,12)

4th Day   The God of All Grace
Ephesians 2:1-10

Charlie Brown was out flying his kite. He was going great guns. It really went up after all. And then, as he stood there holding the string, the kite started to come down. The wind slackened, the line got tangled up, and the whole business came crashing down on his head.

He stood there forlorn, tied up in his kite and string, and the more he attempted to untangle it, the worse it got. Finally he gave up and headed home. He took off his clothes, but he was still entangled in that kite as he stepped into the tub.

The last picture shows him in bed with the kite.

The string is all around him still, and with that characteristic hopelessness all over his round face, Charlie says with that blank expression:

"Years from now when I get drafted, the army examiner will ask me why I have this kite with me, and I'll say, 'Don't ask such stupid questions.'"

We indulge ourselves in sin and at first it seems good. What adventure and thrill! Then all too soon, our sins start coming down upon us. We get all tangled up in an endless string of guilt. "The wages of sin is death": our conscience is hardly at peace.

But the more we tug to free ourselves, the worse it gets! Now we know we can never do it alone. Someone else has to cut us loose, for our situation is absolutely hopeless. We are caught dead in our sins and trespasses (Ephesians 2:1).

The One who can cut the string and set us free does it by the free grace of God (Ephesians 2:8,9). It is the gift of God. It is the love of Christ.

We can never be of any use to Christ, unless we are truly and completely set free by this gospel of the grace of God. Only then can the Spirit begin to use us.

To Go Further

Has Christ cut the string of guilt for you?
Are you actually set free by His grace?
Give thanks for where you have been, and where you are now—by the grace of God. (Ephesians 2:3-6)

Every ad on television must have a note of authenticity about it. If it doesn't ring true, it doesn't last. The best advertising is that which demonstrates conclusively to us that here is a better product, so that we are indeed convinced and "sold."

The people of God need to demonstrate in their lives this authenticity of their faith. Unless we can make it a convincing demonstration, the world will keep on carrying signs which say, Jesus—YES. Christianity—NO.

Part of our answer, the negative side, lies in putting away the sins which hamper our Christian witness (I Peter 2:1):

Malice—which is depravity, deliberate hostility, and general wickedness.

Guile—crafty, deceitful underhandedness.

Hypocrisy—faking it in our Christian lives, living behind a false front.

Envy—destroying our witness by holding grudges and exhibiting jealous tensions.

Evil speaking—which creates division among us by vicious slander.

On the positive side we should be made alive (I Peter 2:5). We must be built into a vibrant, vital fellowship, into a dynamic church that is shot through with life.

What does it mean for us to be chosen by Christ? To become a royal priesthood, interceding for that pagan world? To take our place as a holy community of those who believe? To be a peculiar people in the sense that we are a special people, who are aware that they have been purchased by the Son of God (I Peter 2:9)?

We, who were not a people before, are now by the mercy of God called to be His people (I Peter 2:10). From rags to riches. And if this is Scripture, then we have been called to show forth His praise to that pagan world all around us (verse 9).

Let us become authentic Christians!

To Go Further

Have you become what God has intended for you to be? (I Peter 2:9,10)

How can you?

What should you do about it?

6th Day   **The God of the New**
Hebrews 8:6-13; Ephesians 2:1-10

We have already seen that God can take those who are the living dead and give them life (Ephesians 2:5). Not only has He removed our sins far from us, but He has and can deliver us from the desires of the flesh, of the mind and of the self. He even raises the dead (Ephesians 2:6). He will exalt them in the ages to come (Ephesians 2:7).

Such are the promises of God (Hebrews 8:6). Because of Jesus Christ the old covenant is no more, and a new covenant has come into being. It is a better relationship than the old.

Under the old covenant God was faithful, but His people wandered away continually. Had the first covenant been able to bring about faithfulness, the second would never have been necessary (Hebrews 8:7). But like old clothes that may now be out of style, so the first covenant has given way to the new relationship in Christ (Hebrews 8:13).

What is so new about it?

It is *an inner law*, not an outer force (Hebrews 8:10). It is not written on tables of stone, but in the hearts of men. It is not merely a system to adhere to, but the Holy Spirit given to men.

It brings about *the knowledge of God* (Hebrews 8:11). Not a faraway God who spoke through the prophets, but a God who has come so near to us that He became man and was born and lived and died in our midst.

It is a complete and *constant forgiveness* (Hebrews 10:12). There is no need for the continual sacrifices demanded under the law, for Christ has sacrificed Himself once and for all (Hebrews 9:25,26). Through the power of the resurrection those who are dead in sin are raised to new life in Christ.

And if that is so, what more could you possibly ask for?

To Go Further

What does God really mean to you?

Have you thought about the meaning of this

116

covenant-keeping God of compassion?

Are all things being made new—daily?

7th Day **The Love of God**
I John 5:1-5

She came in from the garden to the study. He sat there behind his desk, engrossed in his work, but she had some flowers in her chubby hand that she had just picked in the backyard. She was only four and she pushed them right under his nose.

"For you, Daddy," she said.

He didn't say: "Thanks a lot, but I don't need them."

He didn't reply: "Look, I don't want you to pick those flowers for me, because they are mine anyway. The whole backyard belongs to me."

Of course not. He was grateful for her gift and so he gave her a little hug.

God can get along without our thanks, without our prayers, without our expressions of worship. He doesn't need what we bring to Him with our chubby little hands and our stammering tongues. The whole universe is His! We cannot *give* Him anything, really.

But maybe, *just maybe*, our worship and thanks mean something to Him. Maybe they mean more than we dare to think. He is our Father, and He loves us. . . .

There is so little we can do in response to His great love for us. But we can respond to Him, even in a small way.

One authentic way to demonstrate our love for God is toward other people (I John 5:1)! Herein we know that we are God's children indeed (I John 5:2). And it may be that our lives lived in love toward one another produce some joy in heaven.

We cannot give Him much of anything, but we can express our love.

To Go Further

What is the relationship between love and the commandments? (I John 5:3)

How can we be victorious in Christ? (verses 4,5)

Does love rule your actions?

Make a Decision

T. J. Neary was a procrastinator. He was always putting things off. It took him eleven years after he had applied for a marriage license to go and pick it up.

He explained: "We had a few disagreements about details."

Procrastination is the thief of time. How many years has it been that you have put off an important, Christian decision? Can you keep on procrastinating? Must you not act *now*, in order to remain a vital Christian?

"They who defend their sin will see in that great day whether their sins can defend them."

CHAPTER 10

Of a Church Awake

"Your brain," said an old schoolteacher, "shouldn't be a cold-storage chamber, but a power-house."

That is even more true of the Christian. We should not be cold-storage chambers where our faith is stocked and hidden away. The time has come for us to be powerhouses, sending out into the world the radiance and vitality of our Christian faith.

That is the intention of the Holy Spirit: That is the hope of a church awake in a world of sin and woe.

Introductory Bible reading for this week: Ephesians 1–2

1st Day Are You of God?
I John 4:1-12

There is an ad which pictures a girl with face cream all over her face. She looks terrible. Her hair is up in curlers, and she's obviously quite conscious of improving her appearance.

The ad asks a question: "Do you think it all happens on the outside?"

Do you? Give some thought to the inner you. Beauty isn't skin deep. There's an outer beauty that wears off with age, and some of it washes off at night. But there is also an inner beauty which shines forth from within.

The church will only wake up when it begins to concern itself with the inner life, and stops trying to put on the stage makeup of an artificial faith. You can't make an authentic or lasting impression that way. And it isn't the real thing either.

So we must test the spirits (I John 4:1). Love is the characteristic of the Christian (I John 4:7,8). If you want to know whether a person is of God or not, you can tell by this test—love.

We cannot create this love. We cannot manufacture it. Love is the result of God's sacrifice for the world (I John 4:9,10). Love comes from the Holy Spirit. We cannot achieve it. We dare not fake it. Only as we concentrate on being filled with the Spirit of God regularly and consistently will the miracle begin.

There are no shortcuts. It takes time and effort, willingness and obedience—commitment, dedication, devotion.

But if you are going to be a genuine Christian, one thing will be necessary. You must realize that everything doesn't happen on the outside.

Give some thought to the inner you.

To Go Further

Is the only difference between the world and the Christian one of faith? (I John 4:1-6)

What does the love of God mean to you?

How can you become a loving person?

2nd Day   Do You Walk Worthy?
Colossians 1:9-23

Someone was talking about going certain places as a Christian and said: "I believe I can take Christ to such and such a place."

Who are you to *take* Christ? Shouldn't it be the other way around? Are you a leader or a follower? The one who makes the decisions, or a disciple?

The Christian church will never become what it ought to become, or be used as it could be used, until we are filled with the knowledge of the will of God (Colossians 1:9). That knowledge will lead to a worthy walk (Colossians 1:10). And the result of a worthy walk is a pleasing and fruitful Christian life.

The strength of the Holy Spirit leads in very practical ways to patience, endurance and happiness (Colossians 1:11). And the ultimate goal of Christian discipleship is holiness, without blame or reproach (Colossians 1:22).

The secret of a worthy life is in this power which comes from above. The actual Greek phrasing in verse 11 is that we are "empowered by His power." God's power is available. We can expect it, and since it is possible to receive it, we are to take it.

"The more we desire, the more we receive; the more we receive, the more we are able to receive."—Alexander MacLaren

There is an old Franciscan story which tells that on a certain occasion one of the saintly Christians invited a young Christian to join him on a preaching expedition. They walked through the entire village not saying a word.

"I thought we were going to preach," said the young Christian as they arrived back home.

"We have preached, we were observed as we walked. They marked us as we went. It was thus we preached."

Although we should also witness with words, there is truth in this old story. Do you walk worthy of the Lord whom you serve?

To Go Further

Pray about Colossians 1:9-12.
Take some specific steps toward the goal of Colossians 1:22.

Some people have a faith that is only good for fair weather. They expect, as Christians, to meet calm seas and favorable winds, without any troublesome, angry waves.

Perhaps they will make it through without hearing the wind howl, or seeing the wild sea show its dangerous teeth. But what a risk to take. We do not know what a day may bring forth. How can we expect to sail daily through life with blue skies and never a storm?

But, suppose, there will come a storm. Then what? Can you meet it? Are you ready for it? Do you have sufficient resources to meet it? If, aboard a ship you need a captain for such a time as this, do you have a captain whom you can trust to hold a steady course amid the furies of life?

When we raise such questions as these, we are again driven to the heart of the matter. Where is our strength? Where are our resources?

Only Christ can lead us. Only He can strengthen us within. Only He is able to bring about the needed transformation. This is what Paul witnessed to the elders of the church in Ephesus (Acts 20:23,24). Because the Holy Spirit was in him even during the times of affliction and trouble, none of these things moved him in the face of death!

He spoke of his personal suffering (Acts 20:19). He shared his guidance to face suffering and death (Acts 20:22). He was deeply disturbed by the false teachers who created division in the church (Acts 20:29-31).

The Christian who has stability in the storm is that Christian on whom other people can count.

To Go Further

As you read through these verses again, ask yourself whether you can affirm verses 19 and 20?

Are you committed as in verse 24?

Can you say verse 26? And so on . . . through verse 32.

4th Day **Do You Have Assurance?**
Romans 8:14-28

It goes without saying that the disciples were expectant men. Therefore they received the gift of the Spirit. But in spite of that obvious fact, they were eager and willing to meet God. That was the key to their spiritual experience.

If we tend to complain that nothing much is happening in our churches, whose fault is this? Wouldn't it be necessary to lay the blame at our own doorsteps, at our own lack of faith, at our own non-expectancy?

God has a spiritual experience waiting for any person who will believe Him. God wants to give His Spirit to any who will receive Him. But if our prayers have become routine, if our attitude has become indifferent, if our approach is apathetic, if we are listless and bored, how can anything ever happen?

The faith which is expressed in Romans 8:28 is not created in a vacuum. It is the result of the Holy Spirit in a Christian's life, bringing assurance and faith (Romans 8:14-17). It is the certainty of the hope that is set before us (Romans 8:24,25). It is born out of the agony and reality of prayer (Romans 8:26,27).

"We know." We do not think. We do not merely hope, but we are certain.

"That all things." Not some things, or a few good things. Not merely the blue skies and pleasant winds, but the fiery gales and the fearsome waves . . . all things.

"Work." They do not happen. They are in reality working.

"Together." Not apart from each other.

"For good." God's eternal purpose.

"To them that love God." An active love, an expectant and fervent love. Nothing listless or bored or negative.

"Who are the called." Chosen and responsive to that call.

Do you have this assurance? It is born of the Spirit.

To Go Further

Put all things in the crucible of Romans 8:28.

Ask forgiveness for an apathetic, routine, bored Christian life.

Pray on the basis of Romans 8:26.

5th Day   Are You Building?
Jude 1:1,2,17-25

Lucy was shouting at Charlie Brown: "Who's crabby?"

"You're crabby!" he shouted back. "You're always crabby! You're crabby in the morning. You're crabby at noon and you're crabby at night!"

Charlie walked away and Lucy stood there almost dumbfounded. Then she shouted after him: "Can I help it if I was born with crabby genes?"

We can always find an excuse if we have to. When we don't like the way things are going, it's amazing how quickly we can find reasons and explanations and excuses.

How can the church ever fulfill God's will in the world? How can we ever wake up spiritually as long as we try to analyze or explain or come up with reasons for our failures?

It is interesting to discover that the New Testament does not deal in reasons or excuses. Christians are not eager to provide alibis for themselves. They are positive in their outlook on the world, and they speak in certainty about obedience, commitment and utter dedication.

Jude suggests in his letter that we go about the task of building things up (Jude 20). It is a building up of our faith which can only happen in the Spirit. He suggests that we pray, that we keep ourselves in God's love and also that we look ahead (Jude 20,21). And if we are afraid of falling, let us place ourselves in the hands of Him who can deliver us (Jude 24).

We do not generally appreciate people who make alibis, because we expect more from them. Nor do we like ourselves for the excuses we make. We expect more from ourselves, too.

So, instead of tearing down, let us proceed with the task of building up—in the Holy Spirit.

To Go Further

What is the assurance of Jude 1 for you?
Will you pray, keep, look? (verses 20,21)
What of the sharing of the good news? (verses 22,23)
Be specific about today.

6th Day   **Are You Concerned?**
I John 3:11-24

It is far easier to spend an evening discussing religion than twenty minutes in obedience to the Spirit.

We want God's Holy Spirit, but we will not meet His conditions. We expect all the results without giving our best. We want a firsthand faith with secondhand efforts.

Christ does not court us. He commands us. He is not impressed by our words, only when we act in obedience. He listens to our creeds but looks for our concern and compassion.

The Christian gospel is one of love (I John

3:11). The demonstration of our faith is love for one another (I John 3:14). As God has laid down His life for us, we ought to lay down our lives for one another (I John 3:16). This is not simply a matter of dying, but must begin in practical ways which anyone can easily understand (I John 3:17).

Faith and life, belief and love go hand in hand (I John 3:23). This is how we know that the Spirit of God is operating through our fellowship (I John 3:24). How practical is the Word of God!

Back in the Middle Ages someone wrote these words: "Do you wish to receive kindness? Be kind to another. Do you wish to receive mercy? Show mercy to your neighbor. Do you wish to be applauded? Applaud another. Do you wish to be beloved? Exercise love. Do you wish to enjoy the first rank? First concede that place to another. Become yourself the judge, yourself the lawgiver of your own life. . . . Do you hate to be insulted? Do not insult another. Do you hate to be envied? Envy not another. Do you hate to be deceived? Do not deceive another."

It sounds so easy, but we know how difficult it becomes to measure up. Not only difficult—impossible! Impossible without the Holy Spirit.

Are you concerned enough to be in earnest?

To Go Further

Do you feel any condemnation? (I John 3:20,21)
Are you willing to confess in faith? (verse 22)
Pray in earnest about the gift of love.

Ephesians 1:3-10

One of the things that annoys me the most about driving on the freeways or turnpikes is this business of stopping to look. Now, it may be understandable that some would stare at an accident, although even that ties up traffic needlessly when you are going in the other direction. Or a couple of cars have mildly bumped each other on the other side of the divider, and you have to stop and look.

Even a policeman who has stopped some poor motorist gets a lot of attention. He may be making a routine stop or giving a ticket, but everybody has to look.

I just sit there boiling within, because the traffic is snarled for miles, while up ahead the motorists slow to a crawl to see a policeman talking to somebody. I'm angry because I'll be late for a meeting, and there's no need to gawk since you can't *do* anything anyway.

Now the church gets snarled up in the traffic jams also. We're always eyeing the side of the road, instead of beholding Christ, instead of viewing the goal, instead of considering the purpose for which He created us.

We lose speed while looking at the minor accident of some other fellow. If only we'd keep on moving, think of what God could accomplish in our midst.

That's part of the secret of living a consistent Christian life. Keep moving! A church that is wide awake looks ahead (Ephesians 1:10-12). It also

129

looks back (Ephesians 1:4). We were chosen by Him before the foundation of the world. The road we travel extends from eternity to eternity.

A wide-awake church walks worthy of the Lord, remains unmoved by the forces of evil, is assured of His mercy, builds in concern and looks ahead.

To Go Further

What is the purpose of predestination? (Ephesians 1:4,5,11)

Have you left the main road? Do you need to return? How can you do it?

Make a Decision

A literary critic once said that the cry of all the world's great literature is: "Read me, do not write about me, do not even talk about me, but read me."

Perhaps that is the cry of the Holy Spirit for the church. Speaking of Christ, He says: "Live Christ. Do not debate about Him or argue for Him, but live Christ."

How?

When?

In what way?

By whose power?

CHAPTER 11

Facing Controversy

Have you ever had the idea that God came to the men of the Bible in very strange ways? That they dreamed dreams and saw visions and then they suddenly had some great religious experience?

Well, that's not the way it actually was. When did God come to Adam? After he had been meddling with that forbidden tree. What about Cain? After his quarrel with his brother. And Moses? While he was on the job of taking care of some sheep.

God doesn't come in some religious atmosphere, but right there in your temptation, right there after your family quarrel, right there on the job. And that's how life can be changed!

Introductory Bible reading for this week: I Corinthians 11; 14

There is an old story about a fellow who gets off a train. (It has to be old, because people hardly use trains any more.) Anyway, he is met with the words: "You must be our new preacher."

"No," said the fellow getting off the train, "I only look this way when I have a toothache."

We have the notion that religious people look like some bluenosed puritan who goes around hanging crepe everywhere. But the very opposite ought to be the case. Despite some of the obviously poor advertisements for Christianity, the most attractive and dynamic Person who ever lived had such a persuasive magnetism that people from everywhere were drawn to Him. They came from everywhere to Jesus.

The church will not be going anywhere, unless it can make a better impression, unless it can put a Christian foot forward.

But how? Through this same Christ, who is not dead but alive forever more. Through this One "who is the image of the invisible God" (Colossians 1:15). He is the head of the church, in whom all the fullness of God dwells (Colossians 1:18,19).

This is our faith: The One who walked in our midst is the Creator of all (Colossians 1:16,17). He who came, is coming again. He who was with us, is with us now. Through Him we can become what we are destined to be.

A refrigerator doesn't just keep things cold by itself. It must be plugged into the power. The world doesn't just run on its own, at 66,000 miles per hour. The power that keeps it spinning around the sun is operative even now (Colossians 1:17).

And what of us? Without power, we cannot accomplish things for God. But with God's power all things become possible. "That in all things he might have the preeminence" (Colossians 1:18).

To Go Further

With the aid of a commentary, study Colossians 1:15-19.

Is Colossians 1:13,14 true for you?

How about those whom you love?

2nd Day **By Prayer**
Ephesians 3:14-21

One of the nation's race tracks now advertizes that if you don't know what's going on at a horse race, you don't have to worry any more. No, sir. There are some very pretty girls at the track who will tell you what it's all about. They're wearing charming uniforms which will identify them, and they can answer all your questions. Horse racing made easy and glamorous. . . .

How attractive is Christianity? Do we demonstrate our faith as the good life? Or do we look as if we had a toothache?

Are we a good ad for those who have never tried it? If horse racing is getting a boost from glamor, how much more should Christianity put its best foot forward? For, after all, those horses are just busy racing around a track. We're *going places*.

This may be a crude way of putting it, but Paul actually prayed that we place our best foot forward. How? By receiving Christ in our hearts (Ephesians 3:17). So will we be rooted and grounded in love. And what is the implication of being filled with the fullness of God (Ephesians 3:19)? The results ought to be far above all we ask or think (Ephesians 3:20).

Our best foot forward.

And the key is in prayer. Prayer is being receptive to the living Christ. Prayer surpasses knowledge. Prayer allows Christ to dwell in our hearts by faith.

To be rooted in love is to dig deep down. To be grounded in love is to lay a good foundation.

When power penetrates your inner being, all that you believe becomes a reality. This is the way Paul's prayer opens and closes (Ephesians 3:16,20).

Let's put our best foot forward—by the power of God.

To Go Further

Have you ever prayed on the basis of Ephesians 3:16-19? How close do you approach this?

Are you willing to change the direction of your prayers? Are you willing to pray in faith? (verse 20)

Charles Spurgeon tells the story of a young boy who said to his Sunday School teacher:

"Teacher, I wish my sister could be got to read the Bible."

"Why, Johnny?"

"If she would, she'd be converted. I wish that at the next prayer meeting you would pray she would read her Bible."

"I'll tell you what," said the teacher. "Can you come to the next prayer meeting, and we will do it."

Johnny was there, and when they announced that prayer would be made for his sister, he left the meeting. During the next class session the teacher chastised him. "It was rude to leave," she said.

"I didn't mean to be rude," answered Johnny. "I just went home to see her reading the Bible!"

Spurgeon concluded the story by adding that she was!

Such is the faith of children. And such should be our faith, too. But we must not get the idea that this is *all* there is to faith, as if faith is a matter of getting special requests.

The heroes of faith did not all survive. They did not all win the victory. When you read Hebrews 11:36-39, you discover that those who are mentioned in the same breath with Gideon, Samson and David did not reap the rewards of overcoming their physical trials. But they lived by a deep faith and so obtained a good report (Hebrews 11:39).

The faith that will not turn sour in the midst of trying circumstances is that golden thread which the Spirit can weave into the fabric of our lives.

To Go Further

Are you able to concur with II Timothy 2:11-13?
Do you trust the faithfulness of God?
Can you trust Him in your particular situation?

4th Day   According to His Supply
Philippians 4:8-20

Parents who love their children *if* they will produce, love the production and not the child. If a child senses that he is only accepted when he achieves something, he is likely to get the idea that his achievements qualify him, but he himself is not really accepted.

The same thing can happen in marriage. If you love your husband (or wife) *because* he does certain things, you love the achievement but hardly the person.

In this manner we may also be teaching our children about God. We may be saying (unconsciously, of course) that God loves them for their goodness and works, but not for themselves. So while we may be speaking about salvation by faith, we may actually be demonstrating a salvation by works.

God does not love us because we achieve certain things. The truth is that we can't achieve anything. We have broken His commandments. God's love is freely given. He loves us as we are. This is part of the revelation of Philippians 4:13. It is also the basis for Philippians 4:19.

Who supplies our needs? The God who loves us, the God who is able, the God who has revealed Himself in Jesus Christ.

What does He do? He supplies all our needs, so that we do not lack (Psalm 23:1).

How does He do this? By His riches in glory. Place your need against His riches and receive that which He can supply. "My God shall supply all your need according to his riches in glory by Christ Jesus."

By Christ. In utter dependence upon Him it becomes possible to affirm Philippians 4:11,13. The person who is self-sufficient, who tries to measure up through his production of good works, will never even approach God.

We are not accepted for our production. We can only come in helpless deficiency.

To Go Further

Meditate on Philippians 4:8.
Can you honestly affirm Philippians 4:11?
What things do you need help for today? (verse 13)

"I suppose you're not going to change your mind," asked Lucy of her little brother Linus, who was always carrying his blanket.

"Nope," he said smugly. "I do not change my mind easily."

"You're stubborn, do you know that?" said Lucy with her hands on her hips.

"On the contrary . . . I'm not stubborn, I'm merely tenacious!"

"You're the most stubborn person I've ever known!" she said.

"I have tenacity! I have the same tenacity that got George Washington through Valley Forge!"

"Ha, that's a laugh," replied Lucy.

But Linus lectured on: "Stubbornness is a fault . . . tenacity is a virtue!"

"You're so stubborn you won't even admit you're stubborn!" Lucy was angry now.

"I cling tenaciously to my very valid view that I am tenacious. . . ."

At this point Lucy couldn't stand it any more. She let him have it. Right in the nose. He fell down as she walked away, and still in a dazed condition from her blow, stretched out on the floor, admitted:

"On the other hand, perhaps I'll admit to a little mule-headedness."

How many controversies might have been settled, without a sock in the nose among Christians, if only there would have been some humility and not so much stubbornness? How many times have we been stubborn even though we thought we were "tenaciously" clinging to some particular point of view?

The problems that convulsed the church at Corinth could have been settled through the God of peace (I Corinthians 14:33). Confusion is not His aim.

Will you admit to a little mule-headedness?

To Go Further

Study the issue in I Corinthians 14:20-33.
Consider the solutions pointed to.
Are you desirous of peace, or do you enjoy stirring things up? Why?

6th Day   Coming to Communion
Mark 14:12-26

Our problems can be met when we come together in Christ. Where there is unity in Him, there will be harmony in the fellowship of Christians. Where there is disharmony, the Spirit of Christ cannot work.

The table of our Lord is the place where we remember His death for us. That scene in the upper room was filled with significance (Mark 14:22-25). It was then they began to realize the weight of the death of Jesus—the value of the atonement.

We often lose sight of the fact that they were

also drawn closer together as they drew near to Christ. They shared in a common cup. They did not have individual little cups. They drank from one source.

The bread they shared was one loaf. It was actually unleavened, and therefore brittle. Each one broke off a piece and took some to eat. The communion they shared, therefore, was a common bread and a common cup.

No one can experience this moment without feeling a closeness, both to the One whose body and blood are herein represented, and to those who partake so intimately in this meaningful remembrance.

We are part of an eternal fellowship in Christ. We join with those who have in the past trusted in Him. We join with those of every race and nation who now put their faith in Him. We anticipate the glorious destiny of the redeemed, who will drink it anew in the kingdom with Him (Mark 14:25).

When this becomes the meaning of the table of our Lord, barriers will be removed, pettiness will be laid aside, and love will become the dynamic force uniting us through the Holy Spirit.

Only then can we stand together against the world's evil and move into that pagan world in united concern.

To Go Further

Think about the Lord's careful preparations for this supper. (Mark 14:12-16)

Consider the disrupting influence. (verses 18-21)
What steps should you take toward harmony?

7th Day   Worshiping God
John 4:19-26

Have you ever seen a flying fish? They're beautiful to watch. They jump out of the ocean, shimmer in the sunlight for a few moments, and then gracefully plop back in the water.

Do you ever think of some Christians like that— like flying fish? They swim around in the world all the time, and then comes church. They get dressed up in their Sunday best, shine for a few hours, and then plop back into their native environment.

You can't tell they're Christians.

Do you think that God is pleased with this flying-fish exhibition? Hardly. The Christian faith means far more than that. It ought to be a reality in the home, at the shop, in everyday situations. One of the purposes for coming together in a church building is to provide encouragement for one another as together we worship God.

Worship is not a matter of going to the right place (John 4:20). Worship is a matter of spirit and truth (John 4:24). Worship must not be in a compartment all to itself, having no relationship to that which goes on week after week in our lives. Worship is not to be a flying-fish exhibition.

If the church will face controversy through Christ, by prayer, in faith and according to His

141

supply, it can then become God's instrument in the world. Individual Christians who come together around the Lord's table and worship in spirit and truth will be drawn closer to Him and to one another.

Then we will be the church. Where is the church? Says Lesslie Newbigin: "Where the Holy Spirit is recognizably present with power."

To Go Further

Consider that these words about spirit and truth were spoken to *this* woman. (John 4:6-19)

Look at her response. (John 4:26-29)

What is God's Spirit doing in you this day? What will you let Him do in and through you?

Make a Decision

She put it this way: "I'm not religious. My friends are not religious. Religion plays a very unimportant role in my life."

What would you say to her? How would you speak with her? What could you do besides talk?

Does this type of person frighten you? Why? Does this type of person challenge you? How? Do you believe that even this person is loved by God, that she is one for whom Jesus died? How can this change your perspective?

Think about some specific approaches by which you can speak the truth in love.

CHAPTER 12

Wake Up, Christian!

The cartoon showed a bum lying in the street. A Salvation Army girl bent over him, as he asked: "Can you save me here, or do I have to go some place?"

We have often been guilty of telling people they must go some place before they can be saved. But Jesus has urged us to go where they are—to be where the action is.

The time has come to wipe clean the board of our interpretations of the gospel and listen to Jesus' words! The time has come to wake up to reality.

Introductory Bible reading for this week: Romans 12–13

143

1st Day   Wise Up
Ephesians 5:1,2,15-20

They bought a new home and they had to land-scape. Since this was his first attempt at a new lawn, he wanted to do it right. He prepared the soil and put in a sprinkler system. When the weather was favorable, he rolled the earth, seeded the ground and finished by artificial light when it got late.

For the next three weeks he nursed the yard along, rushing home after work, watering it daily, shooing away the birds and the cat. In spite of his careful attentions, nothing happened. Not a blade of grass.

One Saturday morning he sheepishly entered the home and told his wife: "I just found the sack of grass seed in the garage." When she wanted to know what had happened, he said that he had planted the kitty litter.

Can you imagine the shock?

Does it sometimes look as if the church is all work and sweat for not much at all? The Holy Spirit is not there. We've got it all wrong and nothing seems to grow.

We have to wise up! We must begin by living as children of God—*actually* (Ephesians 5:1). That means walking in love, even as Christ has loved us (Ephesians 5:2). Only the church that will wise up can wake up (Ephesians 5:15).

What is this wisdom? It involves redeeming the time (making the best use of time), and not going through the motions of planting without the Holy

Spirit (Ephesians 5:16). It also includes discerning the will of the Lord (Ephesians 5:17). And it leads to thanksgiving with worship (Ephesians 5:19,20).

"To be being filled" (which is the actual translation of verse 18) is a continuous process. Not once, but daily. Being filled with the Spirit is a continuing dynamic. It is also the key to spiritual awakening.

Wise up!

To Go Further

Consider the Christian's walk. (verses 1,8,15)
What is the similarity between being drunk and filled with the Spirit? (Ephesians 5:18)
Pray for wisdom in everyday issues.

2nd Day   **Pray Up**
I Peter 5:6-11

There is no point in praying to be enabled to overcome a temptation, and then put yourself in front of that temptation. That's playing with fire.

There is little point in praying that God will convert the heathen, and then give ten cents a week to missions.

There is little point in praying that the lonely may be encouraged and the bored find help, if you are not willing to lift a finger yourself.

There is little point in praying for our homes and

loved ones, and then continue to live in selfishness, impatiently, and with a bad disposition.

Prayer would be a convenient escape hatch if it were only a means to get God to do what we ourselves won't make the effort to do. God does not do things for us. He enables us to do them. God answers the prayers of the person who is spiritually, mentally and physically ready for action—not one who wants to run off to the beach.

The church will not be revived, unless it is willing to report for service.

Peter had this in mind. He told us to cast all our cares upon God, prayerfully, in trust and utter confidence (I Peter 5:7). We can rest the weight of all our anxieties upon Him, because He cares for us. (The evidence of that care is seen at the cross.)

But is that the end? To the contrary: "Be sober, be vigilant . . . resist stedfast" (I Peter 5:8,9). That will mean work, effort, watchfulness and opposition to the devil.

And all this can only be accomplished by God who will "personally equip, stabilize, strengthen and firmly establish you" (I Peter 5:10, *Berkeley*). This is the result of the Holy Spirit working in our lives.

To Go Further

Are you willing to be humble? (I Peter 5:6)
Are you willing to resist? (I Peter 5:9)
Pray about your relationship to Christ and to people.

3rd Day **Pay Up**
Romans 13:1-7

When a person doesn't want to wake up in the morning, it's difficult to shake him awake. Some people don't function well in the morning. They walk about in a daze.

How can that ever change? Suppose they join the armed forces? Then there is no choice any longer. They have to get up. No question. The bugle blows, and that's that.

Or, consider what takes place when they have to catch a plane. They don't have a choice, and they tell themselves that they have to jump out of bed. Most often they do—for a special event.

The church may be difficult to wake up. Why? Because it does not consider itself in the service of Christ, in the armed forces (II Timothy 2:3). Or, it may not realize the necessity of that special event. Everything seems to be going along all right, and it thinks it can sleep in now.

Charles Malik, the onetime president of the Security Council of the United Nations, has said:

"Russia says that Communism will give the common people the greatest advantages, freedom and high standards of living. So you say, that's nothing. If Communism will give him a radio, Democracy will give him a television set. If Communism will give every man an automobile, Democracy will give him two automobiles. You can never defeat the Russians on their own ground. I know Communist leaders. Most of them do not smoke, they do

147

not drink, they work sixteen hours a day, and they are utterly devoted to their cause."

Put that over against a sleepy church.

If the church is ever to wake up, it must not only wise up and pray up, but also pay up. That involves more than taxes (Romans 13:7). It means an awareness of that special event (like the catching of a plane), of mission and service in the world.

To Go Further

Read through the responsibilities of Romans 13.

Are you spiritually lazy? What can you do about it? What will you allow God to do about it?

4th Day   **Look Up**
Romans 14:1-12

One problem about waking up centers in the night before. If you have caroused around and been to a big party, you will wake up with an enlarged head and a sorry sick feeling.

Christians, supposedly, are not carousing around and getting drunk. But maybe they have too many late nights. Too many church socials. Too many committees. Too many activities which drain their strength.

So they wake up without any desire to go about the business of salting the earth.

Early to bed, early to rise will make a church that is useful and wise. The Holy Spirit has not told us to have so many socials, committees, or rotating circles to keep the wheels going in the church. He has told us to work in God's vineyard—the world—and bring the good news to all.

We cannot escape the judgment. We must all give an account for our actions (Romans 14:11,12). If we are willing to look into the future and know that this must inevitably take place, are we ready to allow the future to influence us *now?* In other words, are we willing to allow our faith in the living Christ to stir us awake even now? To influence us?

We do not live to ourselves. We do not die to ourselves. In life and in death we belong to the Lord (Romans 14:7,8).

This honest self-examination of our own lives, and of the church's busy activities, cannot help but lead us into that revival which alone can save us.

If the church is to wake up, it must wise up, pray up, pay up and look up to the living Lord, the Head of the church.

No more of the church activities merry-go-round, but power for new directions.

Look up!

To Go Further

What does all this tell you about human relationships? (Romans 14:4-7)

Are you willing to examine your own life, without compromise?

149

"We've heard so many nice things about you," said the pleasant voice over the phone. "We do hope we'll meet you some day. We haven't been to church recently, although we are members," she went on.

The minister on the other end just listened.

"My husband works hard and he only has Sundays off. We go to the golf course when we can, you see. And he also enjoys fishing. You know, it's really a shame that we are so busy these days."

"Yes," said the new minister, "I know." But his voice sounded a little tired since he'd heard a similar story so many times.

"We'll be there on Easter," she added.

Maybe they will.

But what is life for? All this running around? All this activity? All this keeping busy? Is there no more meaning than that?

"The longer I work with people who need a revival," said one minister, "the more I appreciate those who do not."

Better than a revival in the church once in a while is the steady life of faith and commitment all the time. This is the fellowship that walks in His steps (I Peter 2:21).

He has made the footprints. We are to follow. What does this mean?

Suffering (verse 21). We are not called to an easy Christianity.

No guile (verse 22). No underhandedness, no insults in return, no deceit in our words.

No reviling (verse 23). Do not heap abuse on others.

No threats (verse 23). God blesses the merciful, not those who seek revenge.

Righteousness (verse 24). The summation of all is in a right relationship to God and others.

There's a new way of living for the wise, wide-awake church!

To Go Further

What is Christ really saying to you this week?

What does it mean for you to follow in His steps? (verse 21) How? In what way?

6th Day   **Stand Up**
I Peter 3:8-17

Someone has described the church as a ghetto of indifference. This ghetto, he said, is one of our own making, of our own choosing and our own thinking.

We may not even be aware of our condition. We are so provincial. We stay in our little circles. We move in our little world. Occasionally we declare our interest in a special TV newscast or some issue in the papers. Still, we keep ourselves safely disengaged from the complexities of problems without solutions.

When the church simply looks at itself, it tends to become ingrown. When it refuses to consider the world for which Christ died, it loses its reason for being.

We know that the answer to the needs of all men lies in Christ. If we *really* know this, living and sharing the gospel will not be a burden but a joy. Not a problem but a solution. Not a task but a privilege. We will be made ready to answer those who ask about our hope in Christ (I Peter 3:15).

How? "Sanctify the Lord God in your hearts" (verse 15). Be open to the Spirit of God. Let Him have His way with you. Desire consciously and deliberately to do His will. Seek first the kingdom of God. This is the meaning of verse 15.

A good conscience is also necessary (verse 16). And suffering for Christ may be a part of our experience (verse 17).

How consistently the New Testament keeps on showing the world to us! Keeps on encouraging us to proclaim the gospel!

The wide-awake church will wise up, pray up, pay up, look up and live up. But it will also have to stand up to be heard and seen and reckoned by men. "A city that is set on an hill cannot be hid" (Matthew 5:14).

To Go Further

Is I Peter 3:8 a reality in your life?

Are you meeting the conditions of verses 15,16?

Are you willing to be used to give a reason for the hope within you? Even on this day?

A man who was very enthusiastic about his hobby of skin diving once said to me: "If once you'd try it, you'd be hard to stop."

He could see I was a bit hesitant. But he was right in what he said. If ever I would have gotten started, I'd be hard to stop.

When you get enthused about some sport, some hobby, some activity, you're probably hard to stop.

If you really fall in love with someone, your marriage will be hard to stop, too.

Once you believe in God and take Christ as your Saviour, once you begin reading the Bible and worshiping in church, once you take prayer and meditation seriously, are you hard to stop?

Kierkegaard says that one solitary human being can be a profound influence for God. Reformation does not proceed from numbers, but from one dedicated person. You can be that person. All you need do is take God seriously. If you really do, you should be hard to stop.

Begin here. Consider the dedication of your body to Christ (Romans 12:1). It is the result of knowing what He has done for you in mercy. But it shows itself in various, concrete ways.

Sober thinking (Romans 12:3): A right evaluation of yourself. No inflated ego.

Acceptance of gifts (Romans 12:6): Knowing that what you possess is from God.

Honest love (Romans 12:9): No hypocritical love, but honest and true.

Humility (Romans 12:10): Putting others above you.

Industrious activity in the world (verse 11).

Fervent (verse 11): Zealous Christian living.

Joy (verse 12): The joy that sees through the suffering to ultimate hope and victory.

Patience (verse 12).

Prayer (verse 12).

The person that reaches up will be awakened.

To Go Further

Pray for revival to begin in you.

Vow to become that one person who is dedicated, usable, willing to belong to Him—utterly!

Make a Decision

If you don't plant flowers in your yard, what will you have? Weeds.

To make no choice is the worst choice.

"The hottest places in hell are reserved for those who, in a period of moral crisis, maintain their neutrality" (Dante).

He was commenting on indecision and procrastination.

No choice is a bad choice. No choice is the worst choice. The time has come to wake up to reality!

If you don't plant flowers, you'll have weeds.

CHAPTER 13

The Gospel of Hope

Hope is not a pathetic waiting for something to turn up. It is not indulging in sentimental daydreams, nor is it building castles in the air.

It is *Christian* hope, hope based on the revelation of God in Jesus Christ, rooted in the past, certain of the future, strength in the present storms.

Our hope becomes a reality through the Holy Spirit, who is ever at work reviving the church. "Hope we have as an anchor of the soul" (Hebrews 6:19).

Introductory Bible reading for this week: Revelation 21:1–22:5

1st Day   He Is the First and the Last
Revelation 1:1-16

There was once a psalmist who felt himself tossed by the tempest and groaning on the sea of life. The fierce waves were taking him straight for the rugged rocks, and he was sure he could not avoid shipwreck. And then he remembered: "Why art thou cast down, O my soul? and why art thou disquieted in me? hope thou in God . . . O my God, my soul is cast down within me" (Psalm 42:5,6).

The God of hope is the God you can count on when you think all is lost. When the ship of your life seems to be sinking, when the ship of the church is being tossed about by the tides of the world, the God of hope is the God who creates hope.

He is the God who has come into the world in Jesus Christ (Revelation 1:4). He is the God who brought victory over death by the resurrection of Jesus Christ from the dead (Revelation 1:5). He is the God whose glory and dominion is forever (Revelation 1:6). He is coming again (Revelation 1:7).

"I am Alpha and Omega, the beginning and the ending" (Revelation 1:8). Alpha is the first letter of the Greek alphabet and omega the last. He is the "A" and the "Z," the first and the last. He holds the world in His hands, and time is measured from eternity to eternity.

Our hope is rooted in what He has done for us, and it looks forward to that ultimate triumph.

156

God's will is being done in all the universe except in this earth, and it will be done here, too.

This is our certainty. This is our hope. And in this encouragement the church should receive new life, to be revived by the living, ever-present Spirit of God.

To Go Further

What is meant by the promise of Revelation 1:3?
How does this influence you?
Are you certain of Revelation 1:7,8?
How does this change your life today?

2nd Day   **He Is Lord of All**
Revelation 4:1-11

He was seated opposite a nice old lady on the train, and he was chewing his gum quietly. She leaned forward and said: "It's so nice of you to try and make conversation, but I'm terribly deaf."

There are many sounds we don't hear. When your radio is turned off, you don't hear all that is in the air, and even when it's on, you only get one station at a time (supposedly). Stations are always broadcasting, but you don't hear them.

There may be many other sounds you are not aware of, even though they are around you all the time. Unless you open your Bible, you will not be aware of the praise that is continuing before the throne of God (Revelation 4:8,11). Unless you are "in the Spirit," you cannot discern spiritual things (Revelation 4:2).

Do you think you can hear the voice of God now? *How* do you hear it? Like a voice that comes at you from outside? from inside? Does it come through prayer, through Scripture, through the church? What about the conscience? Or what about circumstances that surround you, and things that people say to you? Could any of these be the guidance which God wants to bring into your life?

We cannot live by bread alone, but we are to live by the words that proceed from the mouth of God (Matthew 4:4). So, there must be a way to "tune in"—to hear Him who is Lord of all.

"After this announcement, we will continue with our uninterrupted music," said an announcer on the air. The trouble with us is that we keep on interrupting all that heavenly music with our daily announcements. And the commercials (which broadcast only ourselves!) drown out the message of hope.

To Go Further

Can you put yourself into the scene of Revelation 4?

What does worship and adoration mean to you?

How can it relate to everyday living?

3rd Day   He Delivers the Suffering
Revelation 7:9-17

There lived a man in Edinburgh who was a confirmed criminal. He spent much time in jail, but he had one redeeming feature. He had an only child, a little girl who was the very image of his dead mother.

One time while he was serving his time after a burglary, the little girl died. On the day of his release he learned of her death and he could not take it. He was broken in spirit, and he resolved to fling himself from a bridge into the river below.

At midnight he stood on the bridge. Suddenly, for no reason he could think of, there flashed into his mind the words: "I believe in God the Father Almighty." He stepped back. Again the words came. He knew little of God, but he did know something of fatherhood.

"If that is what God is," he found himself saying, "then I can trust Him with my little girl—and with myself."

God delivers the suffering. He reaches into human lives in strange, unaccountable ways. Therefore, those who come out of great tribulation sing jubilantly about the throne of God (Revelation 7:14). They serve Him day and night (Revelation 7:15). Those who have lost their lives for Christ *and* those who have been spared will be with Christ (Revelation 7:16,17).

The God of hope is always with us. Are you aware of Him?

Maybe you do not need a change of circumstances as much as a change of mind. Like the furniture in your living room, it may need to be moved around a bit. Perhaps it needs even to be replaced! Paul put it this way: "Be not conformed to this world; but be ye transformed by the renewing of your mind" (Romans 12:2).

To Go Further

Can you trust Him to deliver you?

Are you able to join in the praise of Revelation 7:11? From your heart?

What specific need is yours to bring to Him now?

4th Day   He Makes All Things New
Revelation 21:1-7

A young fellow walked into a minister's study. He wanted to talk about his faith. He explained to the minister that he could not believe in the miracles of the Bible.

Since he was thinking about going into the ministry, he asked: "Must I believe in the miracles of Jesus in order to be a Christian minister?"

Dr. Phillips Brooks answered him like this: "I won't say to you that you *must* believe the miracles, but I say to you that you *may* believe the miracles."

That turned on a light for that young man. He

160

realized that Christianity does not force doctrines on us. It does not say that we must believe, but instead Jesus invited us to follow Him. We may come to Him. We may believe in Him. We may discover that He is all He says He is. Ask, seek, knock. That is the way to salvation and peace.

We cannot be forced to believe that all things will ever be made new (Revelation 21:1,2). We *may* believe the revealed Word of the living God. It does not seem to us, living in this world as we do, that it will ever be different. As long as we keep on sliding downhill morally, how can we ever go up again?

But the end is in sight. The promise is of God. The Word of the Eternal Lord is sure and faithful. The former things will pass away, and the God of life will cancel out death (Revelation 21:4). We can believe Him (Revelation 21:5). He is the first and the last, the "A" and the "Z" (Revelation 21:6).

To Go Further

Do you really believe Revelation 21:1-7?
How does it influence your life now?
What specifically should you do about it?

5th Day He Receives the Bride
Revelation 21:9-21

When you became of age to drive a car, that made all the difference in the world, didn't it? To get out on the open road, to push that pedal down and to let her roar. To leave all those slowpokes behind and to show off this power which made you Mr. Big-around-town.

Some adults continue to feel a sense of power the moment they hold that wheel in their hands. And little nobodies become veritable tyrants on the freeways.

One question. What is a car for? To show off in? To become a means of asserting your power? Or is it for going places? For getting you to some destination?

We forget all about the purpose, as we are bombarded with this continual jazz about power and more power for cars. Our problem is we have speed but no direction!

Man has a destiny. It is described as the holy Jerusalem, the holy city which has the glory of God (Revelation 21:9-11). The description of it is in the most splendorous terms, including the finest jewels in the world (Revelation 21:12-21). This reveals the value and the worth of our eternal hope, of the reality which shall one day come into being.

There is a place where we are going. The important thing about life is not how fast we go, but in what direction. There is a straight road which leads to life and a wide one which leads to destruction (Matthew 7:13,14). And everyone has to choose which road he will take.

Only this sense of a goal will shake us awake from sleep, from lethargy and mediocrity, from halfheartedness, so that a revolution can take place in the church of the living God. We need a dynamic explosion.

To Go Further

Study the symbology of Revelation 21:11-21.

What difference does this make?

Is there something which God's Spirit has been urging you to do? Are you willing to respond to Him *now*?

6th Day   He Ends the Night
Revelation 21:22; 22:5

A man in his thirties said the other day: "The statistics tend to show that most people are converted before they are twenty-five."

He was ready to give up! He was right, of course, about the statistics. Most people do get converted before thirty, but should that lead us into fatalism?

What if the early Christians had been fogged in by such fatalism? "You can't convert a man over thirty." They would have had a youth movement, but not a church on fire.

We need every youth movement we can muster for Christ, but we need even more desperately a church awake to reality.

There's a scene in "Ship of Fools" where the ship's doctor says to the captain: "I've never been able to accept death, no matter how many times I've seen it. In a dream I dreamed I was dead, and I said: 'I can't be dead. I haven't lived.'"

And the captain asks wistfully: "Who *has?*"

Such people are existing all around the church. They ask questions about meaning and reality and destiny, and they do not know the answers. But we know where God is going, and we know where the world is headed. It is a new city (Revelation 21:24-27). It is a new life (Revelation 22:3-5). He makes all things new. He ends the night.

Men do not give themselves greatly unless it is for a great purpose. What can be finer than this revelation, this hope?

Away with this blanket of gloom. We serve the living God. We are disciples of the risen Christ. We can be filled by His Spirit of power.

To Go Further

Let the revelation of this passage reach into the practical areas of your life.

Let the vision give you faith, hope, love.

Become more open to God's living Spirit.

7th Day   He Comes Again
Revelation 22:6-14; I Peter 5:6-11

While her little brother sat gazing into a balloon which doubled for a crystal ball, Lucy came upon him reading a paper as well.

"Fantastic," she said. "Have you ever known anyone who has the gift of prophecy?"

"Just myself," answered her brother.

"You?!" she asked incredulously.

"Absolutely. I can predict what an adult will answer when he or she is asked a certain question. If you go up to an adult and say, 'How come we have a mother's day and a father's day, but we don't have a children's day?' that adult will always answer, 'Every day is children's day!' It doesn't matter what adult you ask. You will always get the same answer. It is an absolute certainty!"

"I'll try it on grandma," said Lucy as she left the room. "Grandma, how come we have a mother's day and a father's day, but we don't have a children's day?"

"Every day is children's day," answered grandma.

Lucy returned. "The gift of prophecy," said her little brother, triumphantly.

There's a little more to prophecy than that. The Word of God reveals the things which shall surely come to pass (Revelation 22:6), including the return of Christ (Revelation 22:7).

We are to look for the fulfillment of prophecy in faith and obedience (Revelation 22:14). In this way we glorify God (I Peter 5:11).

He who lives in hope, lives for the certainty of the return of Christ. And he who expects the return of Christ lives by that power which can change lives now.

The #1 issue for the Church of the living God is to be filled with the dynamite of the Spirit. So may the Church explode in loving concern for our world.

To Go Further

"Search me, O God, and know my heart:
Try me, and know my thoughts:
And see if there be any wicked way in me,
And lead me in the way everlasting."

Psalm 139:23,24

Make a Decision

"If all the sleeping folk will wake up,
And all the lukewarm folk will fire up,
And all the disgruntled folk will sweeten up,
And all the depressed folk will look up,
And all the estranged folk will make up,
And all the gossipers will shut up,
And all the true soldiers will stand up,
And all the church members will pray up,
Then revival and awakening are here!"

"Awake, O sleeper, and rise up from the dead; and Christ shall give you light" (Ephesians 5:14).*

*Scripture quoted from *Living New Testament, Paraphrased,* by Kenneth N. Taylor, is copyrighted by Tyndale House Publishers, 1967, and is used by permission.